A Foreign Port Of Entry

A Collection of Travel Adventures From Asia to the Heart of Africa

RICHARD H ROGERS

A Foreign Port of Entry

A foreign port of entry (POE) is where one may lawfully enter a country. International airports are usually ports of entry, as are road and rail crossings on a land border and major seaports.

ISBN: 9798854441650 (paperback)

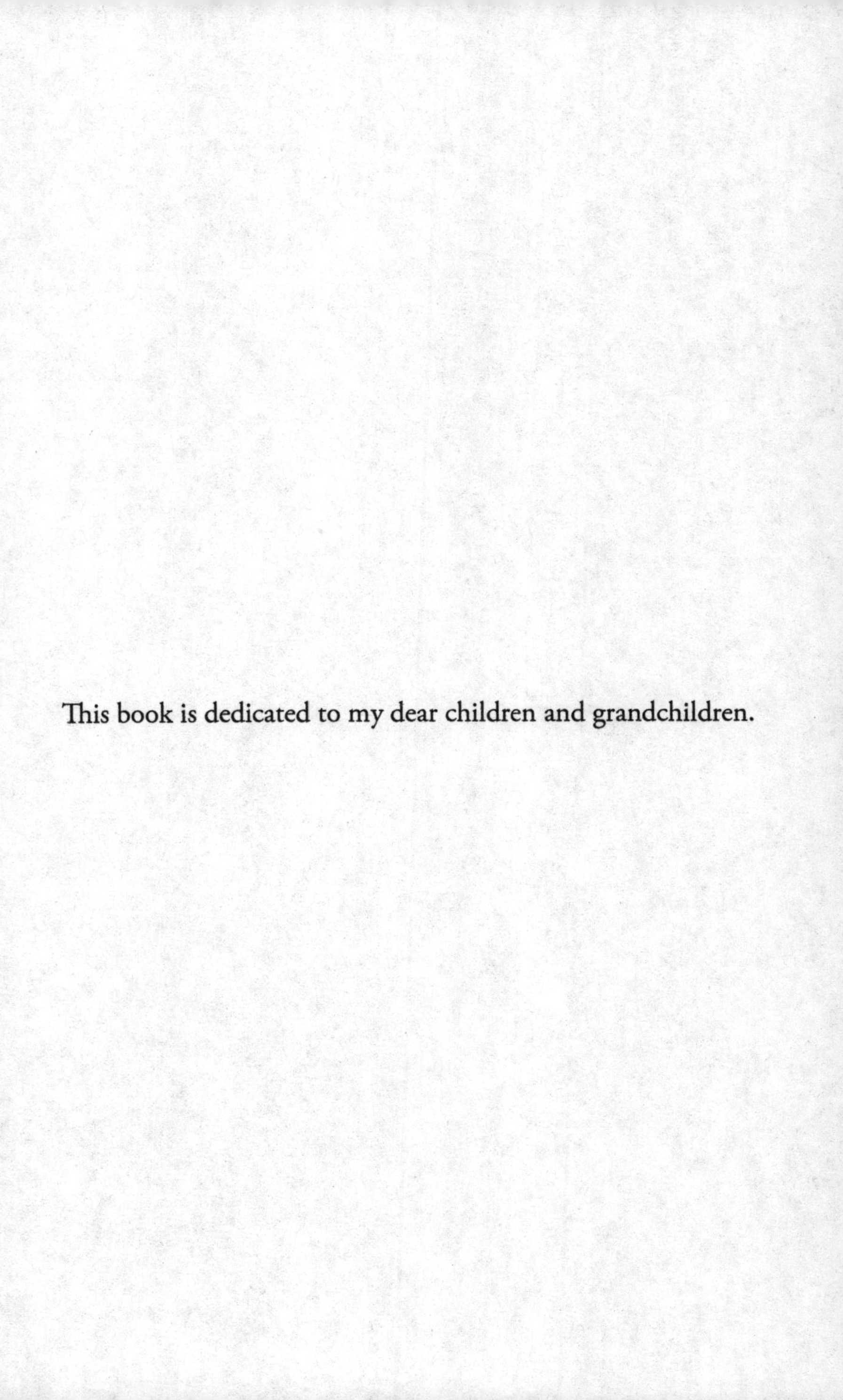

This book is dedicated to my dear children and grandchildren.

TABLE OF CONTENTS

Introduction

A Foreign Port of Entry is an anthology of short stories about my travels through Asia, the Middle East, and Africa. It was not a sightseeing trip or tourist expedition, "see the world while you can." Those were the tours I would probably never return from because, out of desperation, I would have thrown myself into the Bosphorus or given myself away to hungry alligators looking for their next victim along the Congo River.

As an international businessperson, I focused on developing countries. I established or strengthened our existing foreign trade channels by negotiating sales agreements, recruiting new companies, and establishing new sales channels. Due to the nature of my business transactions in developing countries, I did not travel to Paris, London, Vienna, or Rome. Instead, I worked where business opportunities made sense.

The environment was often challenging, never easy, and tricky to navigate. However, I enjoyed it immensely, but one must have the intestinal fortitude to work in such a setting. Having spent my formative years in the Congo, I found that business in developing countries was right up my alley. In fact, it was a perfect fit.

Near the end of my book, I devote a few paragraphs to off shore business development's unique characteristics.

Whenever I have departed from non-fiction, I have labeled my work as a "Short Story." Sometimes, even my fiction bleeds into non-fiction. I'll let you decide if it's unavoidable. All of the stories I included took place while negotiating business in Vietnam, China, Taiwan, South Korea, Egypt, Morocco, Lebanon, Dubai, Turkey, South Africa, and India. One exception, the one anomaly, is the Democratic Republic of Congo (formerly Zaire). As a young, impressionable high-school student, I was less than eager to attend the only English-speaking school in the capital and perhaps the entire country, the only missionary school. As the family's Congo tour ended, I had seen and experienced more than I was prepared for. I desperately wanted to be on the next Pan American flight departing anywhere in the world.

My mind has returned to those days in the Congo fifty years ago, at least partly. My memories have softened with time, naturally. Even so, those days remain vivid to this day. My experiences deep in the heart of darkness have inspired me to compile a collection of anecdotes and stories. In retrospect, it was indeed a memorable experience. This is something I hope you'll enjoy.

I invite you to join me on my visits to China, from Beijing to Quandong and the Sichuan provinces. We had many exciting and mysterious meals, including one open-air, late-midnight dinner, while in Chengdu as guests of local CCP officials. We had delicious, fiery hot Sichuan beef washed down with repeated shots of a local, high-octane drink. I still have some of that liquid as a souvenir at home. However, I use it to clean my kitchen floor. It worked well.

I visited Hanoi for the first time and revisited Saigon (Ho Chi Minh City). No surprise that my stories focus on several grand hotels in both cities. These recall France's profound cultural influence on this country and the region. On a quick business trip to Taiwan, I had a memorable lunch at a world-renowned dumpling restaurant *Din Tai Fung*. Truly incredible food. More soup dumplings, please! I missed seeing Tom Cruise, who I understand was there a while back. Later, I had tea at General Chiang Kai-shek's home. The general was nowhere to be seen.

Istanbul, Turkey, once a favorite haunt of the legendary British double agent Kim Philby, as well as perhaps the best-known master spy, James Bond, and a host of other spy novelists, remains a fascinating city full of intrigue. When meeting your contact for the first time, I always remind visitors that it's advisable to be prudent as you don't want to run into a knife in some dark alley. You will be found floating in the Bosphorus. It can be a messy business and ruin your trip. I recount a quick evening ferry ride across the inky Bosphorus from Istanbul's European to the Asian side. Our small boat dodged giant freighters on their way to the Black Sea and beyond. On the Asian side, nestled in the hills, I recounted a delicious seafood dinner with a dear customer and friend. Istanbul remains a mysterious city with a past that only spies could appreciate. Upon arriving on the Asian side, I marked a bench with chalk, signaling I was ready for dinner. Culinary tradecraft is so essential.

Traveling down to Southern Turkey, I visited our customer in Izmir. Then we traveled to a beautiful quaint seaside town on the Aegean Sea, near the Greek islands. I met a fellow compatriot and a professional basketball star in a small hotel facing the waterfront. Small world indeed.

Cairo, Beirut, and Dubai differ as night and day. The Middle East represents cultures that go back centuries. As an observer, it's fascinating to see how traditions and centuries of history merge seamlessly with the present. Witness the pyramids at Giza and Cairo. With its rich, tragic, violent past, Beirut effortlessly mixes history with tomorrow's progress. To be sure, Beirut has an undeniably European flair to it. Dubai, the shining city on a hill, is a stunning futuristic example of what can be achieved when cost is not paramount. Dubai is surreal and everyone must see it at least once.

Lastly, a note about India: To say I know or even pretend to understand this amazing, spiritual, and picturesque country is presumptuous. While I may have been to India more than a half-dozen times, I realize how few things I truly know and how much I want to learn and better understand India each time I leave. It is a beautiful country with a mystical spirit that I cannot deny. On the one hand, it is a country with the technology and intellectual capacity to launch a satellite into space. It may one day, and relatively soon, have one land on the moon. It is also a country where I have seen levels of abject poverty like I have not seen since my Congo days. The food is complex and outrageously delicious, with a blend of spices that will leave your mouth watering in disbelief and wanting more. For me, it was the ultimate culinary adventure. India is an enchanting, mysterious, and diverse country, from the north in Kolkata to Delhi, then to Mumbai and Chennai in the south. India is forever in my mind, and the pull to return grows stronger.

Finally, as I did with my first book, *A Long Look Back*, I have included a collection of delicious and exciting recipes I have uncovered or enjoyed over the years; I hope you enjoy them as well. The selections include Vietnamese Grilled Chicken with Lemongrass; Lobster Green Curry or *Istakoz* Curry from Turkey; Moroccan Chicken or *Poulet à la Marocaine*; Lebanese Tabouleh Salad; Chicken in Peanut Sauce-Congo-Style; Ostrich Pie from Cape Town and a Madras-Style Fish Curry from India.

Enjoy!

VIETNAM

The conquest of Vietnam by France began in 1858 and was completed by 1884. It became part of French Indochina in 1887. France continued to rule until its defeat in 1954, when the country was divided into North and South halves. Communist North Vietnam eventually defeated the anti-communist South in 1975, ending the Vietnam War. The country's economy stagnated until 1986 before introducing a more market-based economy.

Hanoi in Real-Time

I've stepped into another world. It's monsoon time in Vietnam, yet life continues quite normally. Perhaps, but not for this drenched chicken.

Outside, the rain is beating down with tremendous force, and the wind is blowing, so not exactly my cup of tea for exploring. My hotel is in the Old Quarter rather than the pricier downtown business area. For some insane reason, I wanted a different look and feel. I got that and more.

The hotel staff are amiable and seem super excited and giggly at the prospect of exercising their English with this tall, strange

American dude. One young lady with excellent English skills acted as the hotel czarina and ushered me up the elevator to the fifth floor. I found a nicely appointed room with a flat screen, a large shower room, and all the amenities. I asked about AC as I was dripping and puddling on the floor. The room was over-heated, which only helped if you were in the U.S. in wintertime. She pointed to an AC unit strapped to the wall. Not fantastic, but OK. If I contorted my body, I could have a nice view from a little window of Hanoi's rooftops.

The following day, I woke up to a voice from outside, over a megaphone blaring in Vietnamese. For a moment, I thought they were saying they were looking for a Westerner, a round eye, a tall white American, and the authorities wanted him. Or maybe someone lost their cat or dog. I was answering the question: What's for dinner?

Old Hanoi

Not getting lost in Hanoi is something to strive for. On leaving my hotel, I was given a card with the hotel's name, address, and phone number. This was just in case the crazy round-eye somehow got lost in this oriental maze, this casbah, this Asian souk where the only English spoken was by an occasional tourist. You wearily left your hotel, then found yourself deep in old Hanoi. It sucked in somehow. Tiny stores surrounded you built one on top of the other; men and women were often seen crouching in front of whatever they were trying to sell. One lady was methodically chopping up and grilling some meat, what we called back in the day "mystery meat," and mounting it on a stick that she would then hawk to a passerby or perhaps an innocent tourist; another vendor was arranging a panoply of fruit and vegetables. I walked past endless rows of small quaint stores with everyone on the sidewalk selling just about anything from plastic chairs to brightly colored laundry hangers. Besides half-assembled plastic chests of drawers, there were rows of hanging bird cages with various chirping small birds. Everything was done on the sidewalk. It was the place to do business.

As you walked by, some people watched you, some shyly smiled, others just looked at you with vacant stares, while others attempted to hawk their wares; a sale is a sale. It was a vibrant, 24/7, open-air market. Occasionally I would pass a grizzled old man wearing a North Vietnamese military-issue hat or ragged army tunic; they would always smile and greet me in broken English with a "hello," displaying the few teeth they still had left. How I came out at the end of this Asian bazaar is luck, I assure you.

Sunday Breakfast with Sunshine

Half of the hotel residents (many were French) were seen piling into tour buses and heading for *Hà Long Bay*, a world-famous site to be seen and just under a three-hour bus ride from Hanoi. I can remember from the movie *Indochine* starring Catherine Deneuve that some of the scenery of Hà Long Bay was stupendous.

I had a perfect breakfast this morning. The Vietnamese coffee was delicious, as were the miniature croissants and the pain-aux-chocolate. Going local, I ordered Pho, a delightful spicy soup with noodles; I asked for my Pho with a spoon, please. I felt guilty, lacked class for not managing soup and noodles with chopsticks. My waitress smiled and said she understood completely; she had no idea how to use a fork and knife.

Going to the Dogs

As I waited for my airport cab driver, I reminisced over an unusual dinner with my Hanoi business distributor. He took me to a three-story-high restaurant where we had a sumptuous dinner nicely washed down with some Hanoi beer and a few unknown after-dinner liqueurs. Over barbecued pork, grilled fish, fried eels, and more than a few delicious crab spring rolls, he asked if I had ever eaten dog. I let my stomach recover for a Hanoi minute before answering.

I told my channel marketing guru I had not. He jumped at the opportunity and said I should try it, maybe tonight, yes? I begged off, mumbling about recently putting my dog down to sleep. But to save the day and allow him to save face, I came back with an offer: I promised that if he doubled his annual sales, then when I returned, I would eat dog at his chosen place; however, it might be prepared. To answer the readers' obvious question: Yes, indeed, my good friend doubled his sales, and no, I have not returned to Hanoi since. When I tell that story to my friends in south Vietnam or to those who now live in the U.S., they all, to a person, turn down their nose and mutter something about what do you expect from barbarians.

The author with business representative, Cuong, in Hanoi, 2014

Turtle Soup: How is it Made?

I was sitting on a small red Naugahyde sofa on the second floor of my hotel, very near the Heavenly Spa; I observed our neighbors across the street. It was a busy family seafood operation that bought and sold all sorts of God's creatures from the sea. Delivery house staff would arrive on motorbikes and empty their wares from Styrofoam boxes. Madame, who was the no-nonsense director of operations and logistics, pulled a thick roll of bills and completed the transaction. Buyers from restaurants and other hotels would stop by, and, in one case, the buyer awaited the last rites of a giant turtle.

After discussing the creature's last rights, the father gave the son some helpful hints on using an oversized nasty-looking cleaver; the cut was sure and final. No more bobbing and twisting for this turtle as the head was cleanly separated. The helpful father held a bottle while the turtle was held upside down. This was so that the precious liquids drained to the last drop into the container. The nectar was shaken carefully (but not stirred) several times then some water was added—cultural wet chemistry Hanoi-style. The bottle was handed over to the son, who carefully washed and scrubbed the turtle; half of the contents were poured over the turtle and into a large white bowl, and the other half was placed for safekeeping. Call it a Vietnamese marinade, if you will. Next time you think about delightful moments in Vietnamese cuisine, remember the turtle that once was.

LETTERS FROM HANOI

A Short Story

"If there were only one place to eat, I would pick anywhere in
Northern Vietnam where you get the French and
Vietnamese culinary fusion."
—Jeannie Mai

Hanoi – Hotel Metropole

The rain continued to come down; sometimes, it was just a drizzle, other times it was pounding and furious, reminding us, in no uncertain terms, that we were in monsoon season. The weather was a repeat of yesterday, the day before, and all last week if one noticed. You would wake up and sleep to it. You were always damp, even musty. I developed an unfortunate knack for picking the wrong time to travel. However, I would add that I didn't care that much, one way or another. The press of my business made the weather only a minor problem. After all, it was only rain. I would live.

Many of the hotel's guests, including myself, felt driven or compelled to ask the smiling front desk hostess a litany of brainy questions such as "Does it always rain this hard in Hanoi?" "Does it rain like this in Saigon, too?" or "Do you know when it's supposed to stop raining?" Or "Will my plane leave on time because I have to leave? They're counting on me to do the BBQ back home." Our ever-so sophisticated meteorologically challenged, probing journalistic questions had been honed, I suspect, from listening to well-coiffed empty-headed men and nicely proportioned beauties, both of whom would mindlessly point at a weather map that looked suspiciously like the map of the invasion of Normandy, and then predict their empty-headedness to the world. As a reply, the lovely and delicately framed young lady with almond-shaped eyes chose only a shy smile and a nod. That meant "yes" to all the questions. Staff rule number one: Refrain from disappointing guests by saying no. Eventually, we retreated to the bar, exhausted from all our questioning. Of course, some persisted with critical follow-up questions.

My fingers had been hovering over the typewriter keys of my trusty well-worn portable Remington for quite some time now, hoping for literary inspiration or divine intervention to push through my writer's block. Yes, it was entirely possible that too much gin had left an Asian imprint on my brain. However, I was not about how to self-analyze. My usual rationale, my clever comeback, is to rhetorically ask what else can one do but drink? This is particularly true during these slow, seemingly endless monsoon days and nights. As I noted, everything seemed damp. I mean literally and figuratively. My mind was getting moldy, perhaps even rotting away in the process. That was the consensus of my ex-wives a long time ago.

There I was with my other ex-pat friends at the bar, a pair of Aussies with an extended accent, a Brit correspondent, allegedly from the Guardian newspaper, a rather hefty German couple who smiled a lot and not much more, and one crazy South African from Cape Town who looked like he could have chewed off your head and enjoyed it. He said he played on the national rugby team, and I believed him. Granted, a few missing teeth and a bulbous nose might have given it away. We naturally found our home at the bar, a watering hole for lost souls in surroundings that recalled a bygone colonial era. We were waiting out the weather and hoping like hell the alcohol would keep flowing. For my part, I held out hope in my stupor that I would find creative salvation, an antidote that would help me put pen to paper.

Allow me to lay my cards down on the table, dear readers. I had come to Hanoi armed with my portable typewriter and eager to camp at the Hotel Metropole on *Ngo Quyen, Hoan Kiem*. Try repeating that to your cab driver after a few snorts. I had this crazy idea of following in the footsteps of Graham Greene, the well-known British writer whom I greatly admire and who stayed at this very hotel and in my same room with its view overlooking the beautiful Opera House. While staying at the hotel, Greene crafted the now-famous book *The Quiet American*. Some will categorically state that the same could be said for Greene and his stay at the Continental Hotel or the Hotel Majestic in Ho Chi Minh City, Saigon, to you and me. Yes, he spent considerable time in Saigon finishing his story. I will admit that much. I wasn't that interested in any cultural pissing contest or what one blowhard might say to another over too many glasses of beer. I knew I would end up in Saigon, so it didn't matter to me one way or the other. Ultimately, I would decide which version of the truth suited me best. I'm pragmatic like that.

For now, I would keep out of harm's way. Yes, the winds would howl, and the rains mercilessly come down in torrents, but I would be safe and sound in the comfort of my Hotel Metropole bar. As some ex-pats felt a need to demonstrate their swimming prowess in the pool just off to the side of the bar, others felt more inclined to belly up to the bar and slug down one cocktail after another. It was as if prohibition was around the corner. Others hungrily eyed the local talent that occasionally filtered in only to disappear behind elevator doors. Yours indeed took great pains to demonstrate his superb swimming skills through mass quantities of gin. It was a feat that required exceptional talent, and I felt I was the man for the job.

The other day I nearly fell off my bar stool. I saw Catherine Deneuve, the world-famous actress gliding through the lobby. She stayed in this hotel (and another famous one in Saigon) during the filming of *Indochine*. She had come back like I knew she should, and I desperately wanted to believe this vision from heaven. So, I did what anyone would do with too much gin in their system. I followed her as carefully as possible, not wanting to stumble into a wall or a column that would have ended the chase. Success at last as I caught up with her just as she entered the elevator. She turned to me. The hunt was for naught. I was mistaken. Yes, she was blonde and stunningly beautiful with eyes that swallow you up, and her perfume was exotic and intoxicating. Except for one thing, she was German, not French, and from Dusseldorf, not Paris. She smiled and politely listened as I foolishly tried to explain why I happened to be behind her. I kept the elevator doors from closing. For reasons I cannot explain, she was not in the least interested in inviting me to take a course in international relations. Deeply disappointed, I grudgingly backed out of the elevator and made a sulking retreat to Le Club Bar to nurse my shattered ego with the help of one or several more "Graham Greene" daiquiris.

According to Mr. Duong, our ever-smiling bartender and knight in shining armor, the Graham Greene liquid concoction consisted of two-parts rum, one-part lime juice, and one-part bar sugar. The little darling comes with a frozen scoop of sherbet nestled in a hollowed-out half lemon. Very nice. Very cute. After a couple more samples of Mr. Greene's daiquiris, one tends to skip the sherbet-lemon thing. To complicate matters regarding authenticity, I learned that another contender was lurking about with a claim to the officially designated "Graham Greene" signature drink. This contender, this black sheep, included a dash of Crème de Cassis (blackberry liqueur), a dash of Noilly Prat (dry vermouth), and a "slug" of dry London gin. It was, by some accounts, his drink of choice. Those who have tried it call it "heinous" or "surprisingly good." I tried it and found that one stops grimacing after the second or third drink. I tip my hat to the first contender, as it was eminently drinkable several times over. And with a smile too.

The Food and Beverage Manager felt a need to introduce himself, and his face lit up when he found out I was American. He was looking to place his resume with a major hotel chain in Los Angeles. I told him he stood an excellent chance. Because what do I know? I neglected to ask him when the rain would stop.

A long overdue word about my accommodations: I would like you to think I was roughing it in every sense of the word and dying of thirst in the jungle, suffering from some strange ailment, living on a rattlesnake or scared dog. That would be far too big of a lie, even for me. The hotel is, hands down, the personification of class, taste, elegance, and old-world charm. Everything is designed to take you back, gracefully, to French colonial grandeur. From the moment you arrive, you can't help but notice the classic white façade, the green shutters, the wrought iron detail, the black

Citroen circa 1930s parked near the entrance, the evidence of dark wood paneling throughout the hotel, and the luxurious hardwood floors. Even the lovely staff are outfitted in period costumes. The walls are covered with period photographs. It's very well done and seemed the ideal place to write. It worked for Greene, and I just hoped like Hell it would work for me. Pretty simple.

That evening, with the monsoon rains beating against the windows and the chandeliers turned down low, we gathered for a private dinner. My star-studded dinner companions, included Charlie Chaplin, Roger Moore, Oliver Stone, Graham Greene, and, of course, Catherine Deneuve. All had, at one time, been guests at the hotel. It was a memorable dinner. Over excellent French champagne and vintage wines, we devoured spring rolls from the north of Vietnam, prawns with lemongrass from Hanoi, grilled snakehead fish from the Mekong Delta, and from the south, Saigon chicken, grilled pork, and many a beef dish – or at least they said it was beef.

HO CHI MIN CITY (SAIGON)

Tan Son Nhat International Airport, Saigon

After getting off the airplane on the tarmac and being greeted by the blast furnace-like heat, I could not help but wonder what it must have been like for an army of young 18 to 19-year-old young men from Wisconsin, Iowa, Kansas, or anywhere else in the US, who came here, on a free ticket, courtesy of your Uncle Sam, to fight and prevent another critical domino from falling. They must have realized how strange it was, one day mowing the lawn for Dad or shooting pool with friends, the next day, Vietnam. These young men were far from anything they could remotely call home. I could almost hear the young soldier's boots stomping on the tarmac, marching to the tune of a barking staff sergeant. Too many movies for me, but they left their mark.

I had arrived from Hanoi on a largely uneventful flight. The passenger across the aisle who kept getting sick until she was out of sick bags might have been considered eventful, even noteworthy. The customs officials needed clarification as to why I needed an extra pair of glasses when I already wearing one. What trick was I trying to pull on the Republic of Vietnam? I explained the concept of redundancy in a fat cat country like the U.S. Both agents looked at me as if I had two heads.

There was nothing particularly remarkable about the airport terminal when I was there. As you might expect, the inside was lovely, hot, steamy, and loud, with considerable pushing and shoving by the Vietnamese. Everyone piled up their cardboard suitcases and scrambled to get their pint-sized grandmother safely home to some numbered district deep in Saigon city.

My suitcase was one of the last to exit on the conveyor belt. Just before that moment, I must have looked nervous because the young Vietnamese attendant responsible for all conveyor belt operations asked to see my passport. I was preparing to tell her that I had just finished being grilled by your Customs officials. However, restraint, for once, kept me from making a fuss and turning this into a mini-international incident. I showed her my worn, thick passport. The lettering and logo on the front almost bleached away from sweat and inside the passport, visa stamps worldwide. This made her nervous at first, then suspicious. I had been down this road before. As expected, she waived her boss over, who looked at the passport, looked at me, then smiled. "OK, no problem, you go." Then miraculously, my bag appeared on the conveyor belt.

My hotel driver was already at the greeting line with his hotel sign, and my name scrawled underneath it. He was there with dozens of others who held various characters, some professional looking, others more like mine, with a name scribbled on cardboard. It's a scene that never ceases to amaze me. It could be anywhere, but I would include Saigon, Delhi, Mumbai, Mexico City, and Cairo. Same drill with the same sea of unknown faces welcoming someone. I was swiftly ushered into the back seat of a comfortable SUV and presented with a chilled bottle of water. Scotch was not included.

Saigon has a different feel than Hanoi—no doubt whatsoever. However, things may have changed with the opening of our US Embassy in Hanoi. While Hanoi is the country's political capital, Saigon is very much the business capital of Vietnam. There is evidence of that just by looking at the many skyscrapers under construction dotting the skyline and the exclusive brand names plastered everywhere. International banks sprout like weeds. Hurry up, folks; this is a city on the move.

At my favorite hotel in Saigon, The Hotel Majestic, I was greeted with a warm "Hello, Mr. Richard, you come this way; please sit down, Mr. Richard." That was the beginning of the check-in process.

The hotel is not that different from the one I described in Hanoi and was also built in 1901. Both are luxurious in an understated way, to be sure, and both hearken back to another time in history. The Majestic is steeped in French history with large murals of French Indochina and numerous photos of the hotel circa 1920s, most likely. A few pieces of colonial history dot the main lounge, and the reservation area includes a well-preserved version of the hotel's own Saigon rickshaw (no sitting, please, adults or children.)

Hotel main hall and registration

In my room, the ceilings are very high, with ornate molding that looks about as French as you can get. Stepping out onto my porch, I faced the latest architectural marvel that, in many ways, represents Vietnam's future. There in the distance stood the Bitexco Financial Tower, the tallest building in HCM City with

68 floors and its helicopter pad in clear view. The pad, I understand, is no longer operational. However, you can sit at the helipad bar, as I have, and wonder what it must have been like. It must not have been quiet, to say the least, especially when having a conversation on take-offs and landings. Beyond Bitexco lay the Saigon River with its endless, hypnotically slow-moving traffic.

My bathroom, with its marble floor, was designed to look like the French colonial days circa the 1920s but thankfully complete with 21st-century plumbing. The door to my hotel room seems immense and must have been at least ten feet high and solid wood. It's not the kind of selection that you would find at your local Home Depot or Lowes. Everything was detailed to replicate the French colonial empire's grandeur. My father would have devoured this and wanted more.

GOODNIGHT MISS SAIGON

A Sort Story

Commerce on the Saigon River

In his famous novel "The Quiet American," Graham Green observed Saigon. "And the heat. Your shirt is straightaway a rag. You can hardly remember your name or what you came to escape from. And at night, there's a breeze. The river is beautiful."

The Saigon River originates near *Phum Daung* in southeastern Cambodia, then flows south and south-east oblivious of national borders for about 140 miles, slowly snaking around Saigon, then with a generously wide turn empties into the *Nhà Bè* River, which in turn empties into the East Sea or the South China Sea, some 15 miles further away.

View of the river from the open-air bar

The Saigon River has an undeniable rhythm all its own. In just a few minutes, even the most casual observer begins to appreciate the river and its sense of mystery. From his comfortable perch at the Hotel Majestic's open-air bar, Jack Dearborn, an international attorney with a Washington D.C. law firm specializing in emerging markets, expertly navigated his second double Gin and Tonic to a satisfactory conclusion.

Although he had just showered and changed into slacks and a golf shirt, something other than his tan summer suit, the oppressive humidity kept beating down. Jack was already well on his way to being soaked in sweat again. Humidity was a killer; eventually, one got used to being perpetually damp and soggy. With the help of a cool drink or two or three before dinner, Jack was working hard to recover from a frenetic day of business in Saigon, one that had started with a meeting on the thirty-second floor of the Bitexco Financial Tower in district one and from there to more visits spread out across town in district 3, 7 and there were others, but he couldn't recall them all. All sections were quite different in their own way, yet so alike that it was easy to feel swallowed up, lost in a swirl of color, sights, smells, and sounds. Confused to be sure, yet Jack found himself strangely wanting more.

It was a sure bet to say that Jack had fallen hopelessly, perhaps even irrationally, in love with Saigon. That's why he returned. It was more than just business. On more than one occasion, he had tried to explain to his on-and-off girlfriend, Billie Tilemore, about Vietnam, Saigon, the people, and the craziness he was learning to love. But it was like arguing with a brick wall. Billie was hardly receptive to leaving her historic home in Easton, Maryland, let alone her golfing friends, the post-game luncheons, and elegant dinners at the country club. She was not about trading her life for someplace strange and unknown on the other side of the world where no one spoke English. She could hardly see herself living in an apartment in Saigon, some numbered district, like District 2, off a side alley barely wide enough to fit a bicycle.

Jack was driven to return, or did he want to escape? For now, he was mesmerized by the river and its slow-moving traffic relentlessly pushing forward to some eventual destination, perhaps around the bend or further into the South China Sea. There was no end to the assortment of intriguing, rusted relics that plied the river's brown waters; alongside the vessels were sampans and smaller crafts, many fragile looking yet precariously overloaded with cargo. The flotilla passed his observation point and disappeared. Minutes later, as if on cue, the river scene replayed itself repeatedly as if someone had put a film clip on perpetual replay. Yes, you could quickly become obsessed with the river, and yes, it would eventually swallow you up.

Let the party boats begin!

Across the river, in District 2, the giant neon billboards were all lit up. This included the ones with the two large Heineken signs that now clearly displayed their luminous messages of hope through hops. Jack knew that the party boat parade would soon glide by. Some ships would be adorned in white lights while others, in contrast, were garishly lit up in blinking red, green, and blue lights like a bad Christmas float or perhaps more like a floating bordello that teased the imagination of onlookers with its muffled thumping, rhythmic sounds of head-aching techno music coupled with the occasional sound of girlish laughter. The boats glided slowly upriver and beyond the port only to return downriver. And begin all over again.

As he peered over the railing down to the street scene below, Jack could see it was still mad rush hour, and *Ton Duc Thang* Street looked, to the untrained eye, like an ugly mass of confusion, an inevitable accident waiting to happen. Nothing could be further from the truth; it was more of a choreographed mass confusion with battalions of motorbikes, motorcycles, scooters, and bicycles of all stripes, usually carrying two or more passengers holding shopping bags, small pieces of furniture, and more. The mechanized wave lumbered forward with unbelievable grace. Jack chuckled to himself, recalling the first time he attempted to

Cross a busy street like that. It was not his idea; at the time, it seemed nothing short of a suicide mission. His pretty Vietnamese interpreter told him quite simply, "Just be the rock," the traffic will flow around you as the water flows around a rock in a stream. Sure, Jack thought. It will take your average round-eye a few minutes to wrap their heads around that little concept. But as he said a silent prayer hoping his insurance policy was fully paid up, he took his first step into the congested stream of motorbikes. It was confusing, the noise from the motorbikes deafening and the smell of gasoline fumes overpowering. He moved forward as traffic somehow, miraculously, flowed around him. The interpreter's warning rang clear in his head: You must not hesitate or stop because you risk getting hurt. Simple advice indeed in this deadly game of chicken.

After a delightful grilled seafood dinner complete with a chilled, charming bottle of French white wine, Jack reluctantly ceded his perch overlooking the river. He strolled down one of his favorite streets in Saigon, Dong Khoi. For some reason, he enjoyed calling the street by its French name, rue Catinat. The road is named after the French warship "*Catinat,*" which heroically participated in the French attack on Vietnam in the mid-19th century.

Jack strolled down to the Hotel Continental for an early nightcap. The whisper of a breeze felt like heaven but failed miserably to keep him dry. By the time he passed the Opera House, Jack was soaked from head to toe. The humidity was a killer, as always. He sat at a table near the front door, and the waiter was soon at his side proudly announcing that it was" Buy One Beer, Get Second One Free" for tonight only. It was that way every night, Jack remembered. He ordered a very chilled Saigon beer. He fanned himself with a menu card and viewed Lam Son Square (formerly known as *Place Garnier*.) The Opera House was beautifully illuminated, and people strolled arm in arm. A few hawkers were milling about peddling Saigon souvenirs that would undoubtedly be well received by loved ones in Dubuque or elsewhere.

It was a beautifully quiet evening interrupted by a luxury automobile delivering or picking up its passengers every so often. The Hotel Continental was officially inaugurated in 1880, and since that time, it has had a front-row seat to much of Saigon and Vietnam's turbulent history. The hotel had been the rendezvous point for correspondents, journalists, politicians, businessmen, and, of course, intelligence operatives of one stripe or another. French author Andre Malraux stayed there in the 1920s when he founded his anti-colonial newspaper *Indochine*. A few years later, Graham Greene was holed up in room 214, finishing his novel "The Quiet American." Greene also stayed at the Majestic, Jack's favorite hotel where he was now, preferring it to the Continental. Working on concluding his two-for-one special, Jack admitted that while this hotel may have had a slightly more traditional Vietnamese feel to it, he preferred his distinctly French-influenced haunt at the other end of rue Catinat.

He forced himself to enjoy another "Buy One Beer, Gets Second One Free." No problem: he would soon wear the beer in this heat. His cell phone vibrated. It was Billie Tilemore. He let it go to voicemail.

THE JADE PAGODA

A Short Story

This was my last evening in Ho Chi Minh City. After a frenetic week of business meetings, one after the other, it was safe to say that I was looking to slow down; that may have been the understatement of the year.

I had just finished two afternoon business appointments, which had gone very well. Having something relatively simple like business cards with one side printed in Vietnamese made quite a hit and may have helped a little in underlining our message that we were serious about doing business in Vietnam. A thoughtful gesture sometimes can mean a lot.

All I needed now was an iced-down Saigon beer, a scenic view, a good meal, and maybe some local company. It always pays to plan. I, of all people, should know that. I popped open a cold one from the mini bar in my room and stretched out on my oversize bed. Soon enough, I was running the day's events through my head. I felt some meetings had looked promising while others promised a lot. A lot of head shaking in the right direction and enough smiles to stretch across the Saigon River, but that was all. Such is the nature of business and especially doing business in Asia. If you hurry to make a deal, you will surely come up short. I knew I would be returning to this pearl of the Orient, most likely sooner than later. My mind drifted. I was tired.

Just a quick nap.

The phone rang. There was no reason for it to ring other than perhaps my laundry was ready or they found a ring around the collar, deemed a national emergency. It was neither. While not identifying himself, the male voice on the other end was polite and sported a cultured French accent with Asian roots. He sounded as if was educated in Paris, probably, at the Sorbonne. The voice hinted at an underlying sense of urgency that would behove me to learn more about a most unusual business opportunity over dinner. He said more would be explained but later, at at a location not that far from my hotel on the Rue *Catinat*. He used that street's French colonial name rather than the modern-day *Dong Khoi Street*. There would be a car to pick me up, he continued.

Shall we say 19:00? I placed the phone down, none too gently; I was tired, wanted a drink, and needed time to think about other things, anything that would give me a lousy break from business. A command performance was the last thing I needed.

By 6:45 that evening, I was sitting in a high-back, over-stuffed chair in my hotel's grand salon waiting for someone or something to happen. A shower and a shave had done little to improve my mood. There's a reason why people don't answer their phones. It keeps the idiots at bay. I didn't like the whole idea, and I didn't like surprises. I'm like that. Don't push me or it's going to be a long, drawn-out ugly evening. I can give you a couple of references, if need be.

"Excuse me, sir, are you waiting on a car?" A sudden scented cloud of sandalwood drifted down, turning me into a speechless moron. I looked up at a lovely, smiling hotel attendant in a *áo dài*, a gorgeous tight-fitting silk tunic worn over wide-legged trousers.

I replied," Yes, I am if it's a Rolls Royce." I chuckled at my poor attempt at humor.

"No sir," she smiled demurely. "I believe they call the car a Bentley."

She was right. Sure enough, it was a Flying Spur, an excellent piece of machinery worth four hundred thousand dollars, if not more. The driver had the vehicle idling quietly curbside, the rear door held open by a hotel attendant. With a sweep of his hand, he invited me to settle into a world of opulence and comfort.

Very quickly, I found myself out of familiar territory: landmarks I had carefully memorized now blurred into a confusing patchwork, along with an ever-present army of impatient motorbikes desperately trying to squeeze in front, in the back, or on each side of us. It didn't matter as long as humanity and machinery moved forward. With each turn, each new street, I felt I was stepping deeper into some strange netherworld. I knew we had gone way beyond District 1, but where exactly? I had no idea.

"Where are we going?" I asked the driver casually and indifferently as I could muster.

The driver glanced in his rear-view mirror, smiled, nodded, and in a well-thought-out answer, replied, "Yes."

My luxury ride finally slowed to a stop, and my door was opened. Stepping out, I managed a friendly "hello" and got no answer other than being casually but expertly frisked. Were they looking for my Glock or a wire? I would have reached around back to pull out my hotel tourist map and had them point out my location. However, I got the distinct impression that any false moves or, for that matter, being a smart ass was probably not going to be a very good move. The building I was led to was seductively low-lit and adorned with Indo-Chinese décor. I felt like I had tepped back in time, perhaps Saigon in the 1930s.

I gave it the old college try:

"Hey there, bud, is this an opium den? I mean, where are you taking me? I hated to sound like the proverbial "Ugly American", but an answer would have been appreciated.

I added, "Just to let you know, my phone has a tracking beacon so anyone can find me if I suddenly disappear."

My phone was safely at the hotel, and not doing me much good. Predictably, I might have been talking to a wall. No chit-chat. I concluded that these guys had some real communication issues to work through. I would have been happy to give them my card any other time. Let's have a drink and talk about it boys, what do you think? I followed my guide through a lantern-lit corridor, then up a flight of stairs to my destination, the inevitable mystery meeting. Was I the guest of honor? Perhaps served as a number 5 dinner special with a side of spring rolls? Or had I gotten unwittingly involved in some sordid mess where the stakes were high, and human life was merely unavoidable collateral?

Approaching the door, my mind recalled my past week's meetings. Could I remember anything, even the slightest detail, that should have aroused my suspicions about who summoned me to this mystery meeting?

There was Mr. Duong, that smooth-talking businessman I had met in Hanoi. With his horned-rimmed glasses, he looked like he had stepped out of some B-grade murder movie or, at worst, a Charley Chang episode. We met at a seafood restaurant in downtown Hanoi, a confusing multistory building with nooks and crannies at every turn reserved for private meetings of the very kind. I never saw his office though he told me he worked near the *Hang Dang* Market in the Old Quarter. How convenient, I thought. The Old Quarter was a maze of little narrow streets and alleyways, an Asian *casbah*, and oh-so-easy to get confused, lost, and swallowed up. I had heard stories of strange and unsavory things in that part of town. Not a place for simple-minded wandering non-Asians with cameras at the ready and a bag full of stupid questions.

I recalled that Mr. Duong smiled an awful lot and was quick to fill my glass with some local concoction laced with snake venom, he added matter-of-factly. Before you knew it, you were lost in your own Hanoi fog, a fuzzy echo chamber where things seemed to move at 33 rpm. Was it interrogation time? We talked about everything under the sun, breaking only to sample more grilled seafood washed down with cold Hanoi beers and more local moonshine. Duong seemed knowledgeable about American foreign policy, economics, and technology and was not the least embarrassed to show off how much knew. Duong could have been with the Second Central Commission of Military Intelligence, better known as TC2. I knew that many had been invited, "a mere formality", to their bureau for questioning, and fewer seemed ever to leave. They don't call it the Red River in Hanoi just because of its high iron content!

Closer to home, in Ho Chi Minh City or Saigon, I thought about my meeting with Mr. Nguyen. We met at his office tucked away in District 4 in the shadow of the port. Unlike my friend in the north, Nguyen spent most of the time listening to me babbled away about business opportunities. I was sitting on a little couch fit for Ken and Barbie, in my stocking feet, and doing my Western thing. Mr. Nguyen sipped tea with an occasional nod to let me know he was indeed listening most attentively. He added plenty of well-crafted smiles that spoke volumes, just not to me. I had that feeling that our meeting was nothing more than a formality. Lull the Americans into a false sense of security, then strike! We were all friends here or something like that. His staff or perhaps his crew, which seemed more appropriate, appeared restless. I wondered why they were not busy doing business deals on their computers or cell phones. What sort of event would have the "crew" pacing like caged animals? Was someone going to have a terrible evening and end up *sushi-ed* and then fed to God knows what was swimming in the murky depths of the Saigon River? My mind raced through various scenarios.

Perhaps, my new best friend Nguyen was running dope or funneling arms to the Saigon underworld, or maybe he had a counterfeit operation ongoing somewhere on the premises, all under the guise of running a legitimate business. What better way to look legitimate than to coax in an American company as cover? Was it too far-fetched? I wasn't entirely sure it was.

Coming to my last meeting, I considered Mr. Pham, located on the tenth floor of a secure modern building in an even more secure office park. Pham's perky little peanut of an assistant moved about on what looked like designer stilts. She ushered me into a plush futuristic-looking conference room equipped with all the latest technologies to connect anyone to anything anywhere in the world.

Pham entered. He looked like the embodiment of a successful businessman. He had also seen far too many Hollywood movies and likely saw himself as the Asian version of Gordon Gekko. Wearing an extremely well-tailored suit that looked like it cost more than a couple of my monthly mortgages, Pham was impeccably groomed and oozed charm and sophistication from every pore. He was not bashful about throwing around American-style slang whenever he could to put me at ease, perhaps even off guard. Hey, he must be OK, I mean he speaks like good English! It all felt contrived, too plastic something didn't add up. It was like walking onto a Hollywood set. My gut instinct told me so, and I tend to listen to it even though it's hard sometimes to avoid its presence. I realized that only someone like Pham and his access to resources and people in power could materialize a Bentley and whisk me away for some yet unknown mysterious meeting. Perhaps Pham was just a go-between, an "arranger" whose job was to soften up the target and ready me for whatever strange, sinister series of events lay behind that door.

My guide knocked once on the heavy oak door, then twice, louder the second time. I heard the distinct, though muffled, sound of a phone ringing behind the door. It rang and rang, getting louder each time. Would somebody please answer the damn phone!

Yes, the phone rang all right, but it was my phone. In a fog, I fumbled and picked up the receiver, only to hear a smooth, silky voice telling me this was my 6:30 AM wake-up call.

PEOPLE'S REPUBLIC OF CHINA

From the 3rd century B.C. and for the next two millennia, China alternated between periods of unity and disunity under a succession of imperial dynasties. After World War II, the Chinese Communist Party under Mao Zedong established an autocratic socialist system that is still very much the China of today—the more things change.

I Arrive in Beijing

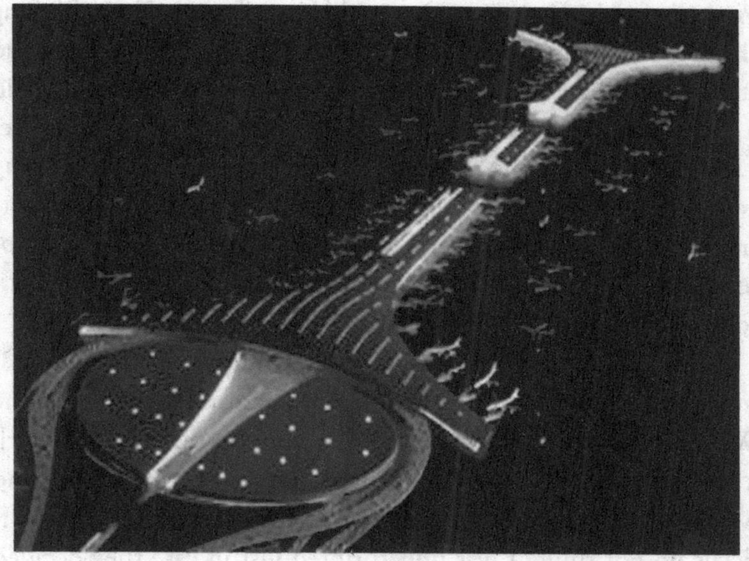

As we gradually descended toward Beijing international airport, the fog of pollution, which had been quite noticeable before Beijing, seemed to have mysteriously cleared up once we landed. Either Chinese officials had put out the word, or a recent sandstorm had helped to clean up the air and drive it out towards the badlands. Someone else could take their last few deep breaths.

At last, with wheels on the ground, I said my goodbyes to the pleasant French couple who were my seatmates for the final leg of my fourteen-hour flight. Sleep-deprived and in another time zone, our team entered the airport terminal. This is a terminal that one should take notice of. I have been to more than my share of airports worldwide, and Beijing Airport was beautifully designed inside, all done expressly for the Olympics. One could be easily fooled into thinking this symbolized a new Beijing and an awakened China on the world stage. Mass advertising covered every inch of wall space, hawking, in a slick style, one major Western brand after another, from the Ester Lauder glam posters to international banking services. Everything is global and at your fingertips. There were no Chairman Mao portraits anywhere. Why mix CCP politics with clever branding, as doing so would only confuse Westerners about the real China? Just follow the bling and the sweet deals, Mr. Businessman.

One soon arrives at a row of unsmiling bureaucratic customs officials, waiting with their official stamps and ready for the Western onslaught. It was neither the time nor the place to crack a few jokes like, "Hey, did ya hear about the guy in Beijing who walks into a bar with a monkey on his shoulder?" Passport officials do not smile. I was fingerprinted just in case they decided to compare it to the ones in my local post office. On subsequent trips, Chinese officials upped their game by first fingerprinting me as I entered the hall, then just in case I burned off my prints or took off my plastic skin hand cover, I was fingerprinted again. I can only imagine what would have happened had they found a mismatch. I suspect I would be writing this from a Chinese prison, between re-education classes and lots of sticky rice with funny-looking crawly things running about.

We were met at the airport by two of our client's employees. They were, as expected, each holding large pieces of school-size posterboard with our company name emblazoned for all to see. Sizing up their Western passengers, they decided one car would not be enough. Perhaps they were trying to divide and conquer us, soften up lazy Western imperialist dogs. By now, as punch-drunk, sleepless enemies of the proletariat, we would have agreed or said anything in return for a bed and a little sleep. Very clever, I thought, so this is how it will be, and I bet my hotel room will have water drip-dripping all night, driving me to surrender and confess everything I know, even my favorite television shows.

My escort was a young man by the name of "Johnson" (clearly a salesman who must have coined his new Americanized name from some TV sitcom personality, maybe he pictured himself driving a cigarette boat somewhere in China). He kept insisting to me that "I speak English but only a little and not too good" typically downplaying any personal achievement for the greater good of the party. He knew enough English to talk my ear off about business, sales, marketing, and American TV. "I lobe CSI and House, and why only one season of Mob Daughters?"

Every so often, "Johnson "would interrupt our meaningful conversation to return to his cell phone and scream at the driver of the official car, the one who kept lagging on China's favorite airport speedway. A factoid that I found rather unsettling is that Beijing has five (not just one like most capital cities) completed beltways around the city, with nine expressways heading in almost every direction and eleven National Highways. That's moving many people 24 hours a day, all year, and still, the traffic is clogged daily. When you think about the Lunar New Year, at least in Beijing, it must be like rats leaving a sinking ship. Masses of people show up at train stations to go home on holiday to be with family. The photos are a sight to behold; it's as if these were the last trains before the invading army arrived. I shudder to think of the visuals of those eleven national highways leaving moving the masses from the city. Far too many ants for me

Going home

I casually remarked to "Johnson" that I might be interested in visiting the remnants of old Peking in the *Hudong* district and maybe seeing the remains of the international powers Legation Quarter, a three-quarter square mile of inner city given over to foreign legations or embassies in Beijing until WWII. I was quizzed, almost reproachfully, clearly I had asked the wrong question and now belonged in some re-education camp. "Johnson" asked me why I was not more interested in seeing things that represented the new, more prosperous

Beijing? Remembering that I was a foreigner who did not know better, he eventually relented and said he would look into arranging a visit. I held scant hope of that ever happening. If it did happen, it would end with a one-way ticket for me to somewhere deep in Mao's China. With my cultural *faux pas*, I was doomed. I could forget about applying to university, and my credit score would be adjusted to reflect my ignorance. Had there been a role reversal, I might have been equally surprised if "Johnson" had asked to see remnants of the 1960s riot-torn corridor in southeast Washington DC. Maybe that's a stretch because I don't care one way or the other, to be honest.

Amidst the drabness of the concrete jungle stood a shimmering-looking structure that towered over everything. I asked "Johnson", "What was that building?" He laughed. "That is hotel our office just next to it." I see; I thought to myself, how convenient can you get? Were our rooms also bugged? I felt like asking. With our team on the ground, it was cheaper by the dozen to wire all our rooms, if they weren't already. Memo to self: Don't look for bugs in your room; assume everything you say is being bugged. The proletariat class does not need privacy.

Standing by the hotel entrance and looking impatient from waiting for us was *Empress Dowager* herself (aka THE client) with one of her lieutenants alongside her. Both dashed to grab our carry-on bags, with the Empress coming up with our president's briefcase while the lieutenant emerged with mine. I was told (not asked) "You leave bags now." I felt I should let them know that our briefcases were not locked, so please copy everything that suits you, especially the "Chinese Strategy" page.

We were summarily escorted to the check-in counter, where customers and staff somehow parted, letting the Empress approach the reception area. It was reminiscent of biblical pictures depicting Moses parting the Red Sea—the same effect.

Passports were collected by nervous hotel employees mindful of the Empress's ever-watchful eye. We were not fingerprinted, which surprised me. I filled out a few forms and signed them, attesting that I was, in fact, a corrupt and spineless running dog of the proletariat and more than likely a spy. In return for my confession, I was presented with my room keys and Mao's Little Red Book (not exactly). See how easy it is to get along in China? To impress us even further, warm chocolate chip cookies were presented. "This hotel signature cookie, you take" and a moment later, we were directed into an elevator with the Empress, her lieutenant, and "Johnson." We were then each ushered to our rooms (Chinese tuck-in service), and I was told, in no uncertain terms:

"You sleep now, at six we go to restaurant and have famous Pecking Duck."

Before they left, I congratulated" Johnson" on his fine English, much to his dismay. They all laughed at this (politely), and I could see it made "Johnson" shrink in utter despair. My comment must have been perceived as taking away the Empress's luster and attention. We are such crazy Americans. Cultural *faux pas* number two. I was on a roll. Could it get any better? Two days later, "Johnson" was invisible. I have no idea what happened to him. I imagined him hidden in a re-education camp, in a province far way. Please don't mess with the Party, that is the only thing I can say.

CHINESE BUSINESS MEALS WITH LOCAL FIREWATER AND SOY MILK

"Anything that walks, swims, crawls, or flies with its back to heaven is edible." (Cantonese saying. Source: The Chinese Kitchen by Eileen Yin-Fei Lo)

One eventually gets used to the rhythm of things in China, at least in terms of what to expect culinary-wise. I'm sorry, but Chinese banquets have some rather scary items placed on those gigantic lazy susan contractions that were first used in 13th-century China as a means of torture. Over time, they gained popularity for delivering food, eventually finding their way into Chinese restaurants as a "hygienic dining tray" in the 1960s. I have checked Amazon to see if they sell them, just in case I want to have some friends over. From my white-faced perspective, hygiene was not exactly what came to mind as diners double-dipped their chopsticks or picked certain foods by hand. Yours included, who had repeatedly failed Chopstick 101, fumbled on many occasions then opted to go in by hand. These lazy susan contraptions go around and around, and where it stops, nobody knows, but you pray it's your neighbors' turn. We are not talking about your local Chinese restaurants where it's egg rolls, rice, Hunan spicy chicken, and a six-pack of Mountain Dew. That's the American version. In China, you are encouraged, perhaps collectively urged is a better way to put it, to try something in a dish that was a big hit with your local team and a hit with the Empress. All eyes are on you as you venture into the culinary unknown. Was something moving on that plate, or was it just your imagination getting the better of you?

Let me pause and admit that what threw me into a culinary loop was the Empress, sitting next to me, tilting her head gently to one side, then blowing her nose out onto the carpet. What small appetite I did have, I fought back a gagging sensation and drank it away. No need for a handkerchief here. Move along, please; nothing to see. More rice, Mr. Richard? Spin the lazy susan, now.

These forays into the culinary unknown were frequently interspersed with toast after toast of fiery rice wine to the cheers of "*gam-bay*" or bottoms-up round eye and likely "long live the Party." It was vaguely reminiscent of my misspent youth after one too many rounds of local red eye mixed in a garbage can in the basement of a Frat house. That's another story.

A word about water: it's a topic to be taken seriously. Everyone arriving in China, at least from the United States, should know you do not drink tap water. Instead, drink only bottled water and no ice cubes if you decide to hang around the hotel bar. That means brushing your teeth with bottled water and remembering not to look up in the shower. Silly? No, just and to be ignored at one's peril.

Here is an interesting example. There was a recent scare (it seems there are many of those when it comes to water) involving a well-recognized water bottling company that sold "safe" water that was not exactly "free" from bacteria. What's a little mistake among the masses, if asked? Did Mao complain during the Long March? Did Ling Biao complain? Maybe that's a bad example, as he died under suspicious circumstances. No one's perfect. Circling back, the bottle had a red label for quick identification, and thank goodness, when I checked my hotel room, I had two blue-labeled bottles in the room. Would the blue label be the next suspect? Would I look forward to spending the rest of my evening shuttling between the bathroom and bed and wishing I was dead or back home and dead?

Tomorrow is our presentation, where some 300 or so serious-looking, no-nonsense government officials and eager students are expected to attend.

Each evening, like clockwork, we were collected at our hotel, hustled into a car, and sped away to another unknown fine down-town Beijing establishment for dinner. Surprise, we were be ushered into another banquet room with what looked like a hundred cute little Chinese ladies all smiling bashfully and saying nǐ hǎo (pro-nounced "knee how" or hello in the lingua franca). I must say, these events have helped my Mandarin vocabulary grow by leaps and bounds. I could now easily say hello and cheers with remarkable ease. Such progress. So begins the language journey of a thousand miles.

The lazy susan, that medieval torture table, was already build-ing up steam as many unknown dishes were being placed on the table, one after the other, everything from raw shrimp doing the backstroke in some mysterious sauce, tofu that smelled like socks that should have been washed a year ago, to something floating in a dark soup, various crispy creatures and more. With the lazy susan, everything moved, and you had to be fast with your chopsticks lest you show what a silly foreigner you are. The food was served alongside tall glasses of warm tofu milk. Having gagged on tofu milk at lunch, I respectfully begged off and settled for a nice cold twenty-ounce Chinese beer. And keep them coming!

We were shuttled back to the hotel and instructed where and when to meet the next morning. My colleague and I took the opportunity to empty a few Gin and Tonics in an expansive bar that was nearly empty, given the time of night. A few groups were drinking tea, and a few young ladies (state-sanctioned and who report on every interaction with a foreign customer) were twiddling their thumbs, patiently waiting for the next lonely guest to walk out to the bank of elevators. A little word to the wise, avoid any glance out of curiosity because that means "game-on." They will stick to you like glue, and you will have to get rid of them in a not-too-friendly manner.

Earlier that day, I had to "cry uncle" at lunch because it appeared our Chinese friends were not drinking at lunch, preferring, instead, the joys of warm, disgusting soy milk, the kind you taste, and your stomach turns and says, "what do you take me for a garbage dump?" They all toasted with it, and I had to fake drink it with a smile as the warm soy pushed against my lips like a relentless wave crashing against a boardwalk. "Did you enjoy it; do you want more? Chinese coffee you like." Don't get me wrong, I may have missed something significant here, but I almost lost my lunch with soy. Yes, I know that sounds like a Madison Avenue tagline, but it's true. And I rather like that tagline. To me, soy milk has no redeeming qualities, much like its cousin, tofu. As far as I'm concerned, soy is a drink for scrawny, little people with bad attitudes who think they are better than the rest of us working stiffs. They have a "do as we say" attitude, smiling and showing their perfect teeth. If the Chairman were alive, he would look down and give me the thumbs up in approval. He was right, Our Chinese friends no longer represented the masses. Long live the revolution! Long live the proletariat class!

A Conference in Mandarin

The official conference took place on Tuesday, and, like clockwork, two black sedans arrived to pick us up and shuttle us to the conference hall. The excitement was already at a fever pitch. The hall was filled with professionals, somber-looking Party bureaucrats, and students, some of whom were trying to catch a few quick naps. That simple act, by itself, could ruin a student's career forever. It could leave him with no option but to disgrace his family, flee to the United States, wash dishes, and work on his Chemical Engineering degree. After that, he would be forced to get a six-figure job, most likely for a company with several sensitive government contracts. He would be too ashamed to let his parents know. Allow me to present the beginning of the last act. At some point, contact would be made by someone from the Chinese Embassy who would let him know his parents were not doing well and needed his help. Wanting to be a good son and a good Chinese citizen, what could he do to help? Get the subtle picture? Further instructions will be forthcoming. It's an old game perfected over time by our Chinese friends. They try and do the reverse and get unsuspecting U.S. professors, business leaders, or persons of influence to come to China by dangling large sums of money. Washington tries to do something like that with Chinese academics though I am not sure we are as successful.

We sat patiently near the front of the stage until it was our turn to present. Up to that point, I had been listening, most attentively, as speaker after speaker addressed, in Mandarin, the assembled faithful on Chinese developments in water analysis and technology, each with their full slide deck and showing us just how well they could work with their little red pointers. By the time we broke up for lunch, I was almost fluent in Mandarin and wanted a damned pointer.

For lunch, we had, well, we had Chinese food. Then we returned for another three hours of presentations, slides, and dancing red pointers. And more tea, as always, served by stern-looking, unsmiling women with severe haircuts and wearing Mao-style jackets. I had to say, "I just loved the look!" I inquired if they preferred Seinfeld or The Love Boat. No answer, just a warm look suggesting that maybe a special re-education camp was possible in my future.

The state dinner that evening was at yet another restaurant, but this time with a sprinkling of key government officials in attendance, all in ill-fitting dark suits and wearing their best somber-looking poker faces. All had conveniently forgotten their business cards. But did we? Not us, sir; here you go, guys, one for you and you. Anything else you want, keys to the Kingdom perhaps, access to our top technologies maybe? Oh wait, you already have those. It was an enjoyable evening eating more of the unknown and belting down more rice wine only to build up a better Chinese headache, better for weak deal-making. So, smart these party officials.

I learned that my colleague had been down for the count since early that following morning. While nursing a Chinese headache, he took a glass of tap water from his hotel room. It could also have been one of those little creatures he ate, much to the amusement of all our guests (that crazy American will be one sick dude.) Now we know how to defeat the Americans, high-five, and *gam-bay* to that brother. The hotel doctor worked his magic; however, my sick comrade in arms will not attend the evening's festivities. Lucky man. I recall a near-miss on one occasion, arriving in Beijing, I was disoriented, having been locked away for 15hrs in a pressurized cabin, in several time zones, and just maybe a few too many glasses of wine. Once in the terminal, there was an elegantly designed "Fresh Water" fountain almost calling my name; I was weak; I succumbed and drank from it as if I had found an oasis in the desert. I stopped mid-way, suddenly realizing I was signing my own death warrant. How soon before the Chinese bacteria start their long march to my intestines? Nothing happened. I was stupid lucky.

We are off to visit the Great Wall of China tomorrow very early. We have been permitted to have Friday night off before our departure and the start of the next leg of this most exciting trip. *nǐ hǎo* y'all. All I want is a good night's sleep. And a Chinese cheeseburger. They can copy our intellectual property to near perfection, but they have a significant problem putting together a hamburger between two buns. Go figure.

Learning Mandarin

*N*ear the end of one of my numerous trips to China, my colleague and I, on this visit, were invited to a product presentation highlighting several of the major players in the drinking water distributor/purification market space in China: no small territory and colossal business. By now, we were accustomed to being "handled" by our Chinese partners. They have a way of doing things that can be maddening as Hell to a Westerner, or maybe it's just me. Impossible.

It was an instructive afternoon, and since the presentation was held in a hotel, it was just a matter of an elevator ride up to our dining facilities. Standard Operating Procedures. By now, dear reader, you know or imagine what lies ahead. Over dinner, using my chopsticks to grab what I could from the lazy susan from Hell, I noticed an attractive Chinese lady clearly commanding the attention of her colleagues and other nearby dinner guests. My local Chinese-US-based partner informed me that the lady in question was the marketing director for one of China's largest water purification companies. She also received several thousand acres of land courtesy of the state, shall we say? Let me add that she just happened to be a close friend of the wife of the leader of the Chinese Communist Party (CCP). That's right.

That following day, my colleague, who had risen from the dead, and I embarked on a tour of a water purification plant in Beijing proper but at quite some distance from our location. The industrial park appeared empty, and we drove for miles until we finally reached the plant. My language education was about to begin. As we gathered, the lady from last night's dinner demanded my attention in Mandarin (indeed not my go-to language), pointed to a conveyor belt, and said "conveyor belt" in Mandarin. She then looked at me. I didn't know if I should say, "Sorry, I'm busy tonight," but I quickly figured I had to parrot the name back in my best Mandarin accent. At times, a word such as "conveyor belt," "cleaning system," or "gallon water bottles" had three or more words in Mandarin all linked together. I dutifully repeated what I thought I heard, and the teacher either nodded and smiled at my progress, or she vigorously shook her head and repeated the word. "Why so stupid?" she seemed to be saying in Mandarin but with a smile. This went on throughout the plant tour. Why me? I didn't have the slightest clue or wish to pursue it further. When we left the plant, I was mentally exhausted and accused by my colleague of having shamelessly cozied up (he used a more direct term) to a Communist customer. I told him I would do anything to grow my market share.

To Canton by Train

After a fourteen-and-a-half-hour flight from Washington, DC, to Beijing, China, only to catch a three-and-a-half-hour flight further to Hong Kong, it was safe to say I could have been in a more pleasant mood and thoroughly disoriented. I was a walking, talking vegetable. Arriving at the hotel at ten in the evening, we were due to depart by bullet train to Canton the next day. My room, which was on the 50th floor or possibly higher, afforded me a breathtaking view. Hong Kong's Kowloon Bay, viewed by night or day, was truly mesmerizing.

Soon enough, we were aboard the Hong Kong-Shenzhen-Guangzhou high-speed train, which, I will admit, is a slick piece of machinery. I was comfortably ensconced below deck and ready for a trip that would take seventy minutes of sleep to cover 120 km or 75 miles. A stern-faced, official-looking attendant wheeled her cart down the aisle. I thought I recognized her as one of the tea ladies who served me tea at the conference in Beijing. Maybe they were sisters; I should have asked. I would have recognized that early-Mao glam look anywhere. Her cart held bottled water, which was handed out to each passenger. I accepted but decided not to drink the water without knowing the safe color cap of the day. Why play Chinese Roulette? I also begged off purchasing any of the other goodies in her cart. I was going to play it smart, at least this time, and give my stomach a rest.

I had plenty of time to look out my window at some remarkably uninteresting scenery. I quickly grew tired of seeing high-rise building complexes, one after the other, that seemed empty, awaiting the arrival of the masses. The drab, colorless view left me feeling numb and depressed. All I could think of was a sign I used to see somewhere along US Route 95 that read: "If you lived here, you'd be home by now." But I didn't live here, nor did I want to, and this was not a place I could ever call home.

With the gentle sway of the speeding train, I fell into a much-needed deep sleep. I dreamt I was forcefully given a severe Chinese-style haircut and presented with a cup of tea by a lady in a blue smock, a severe haircut, and a toothless smile. Where could all of that have come from?

Call it Canton or Kwangchow or Guangzhou, for that matter. Whatever strikes your fancy, remember that Guangzhou, on the Pearl River, is the capital and largest city in Guangdong province in South China. It is also the third largest city in China, so I expected no dusty dirt roads nor quaint Chinese scenery and little houses tucked in mysterious narrow alleyways lit by Chinese lanterns. Even though I had no preconceptions, I was amazed at how vibrant and alive this city was. I had to find a taxi to take me across town to my hotel. The week ahead would be jam-packed with time spent at the convention center alongside thousands of people. So cozy. Our evenings would be spent, chopsticks in hand, gathered around a familiar lazy susan filled with unrecognizable food items. In a few days, we would be at Guangzhou airport on our way to Chengdu, in Sichuan province. More adventures lay ahead.

Midnight Dinner Somewhere in Sichuan Province

"I love the masochistic aspect of eating seething real Sichuan food in Sichuan Province," Anthony Bourdain.

There we were, my colleagues and I, our customer and our translator, all comfortably squashed between suitcases, briefcases, and laptops inside a small van built for a family of four Chinese or two Americans. The van had seen better days. Our driver grinned, proudly showing us his few remaining teeth. "Are we somewhere, perhaps in Hell?" I asked. He smiled, nodded, and said, "Yes, hotel." He was a rural road warrior and showed no fear as he slammed into gear, and off we headed in a cloud of blue smoke and belching exhaust, down one strange road after another. Our road trip took us further away from Chengdu, home to the famous Chengdu Research Base of Giant Panda Breeding, towards our destination, Meishan City.

We had left the airport at Guangzhou for our destination, the airport at Chengdu, hours ago, or so it seemed, having first cooled our heels for over three hours due to a pea-soup-like fog and driving rain. We were all socked in and waiting for the weather to break. Since dinner time drew near, our airline, conscious of the wait, offered up ready-made dinners to appease the hungry revolutionary masses ready to waive their little red books in protest.

Almost crushed by the human wave, excited at the prospect of a free meal, I fought to the counter to collect my dinner, one small bottle of water, and my requisite chopsticks. I don't know what possessed me, perhaps the continued lack of a good night's sleep, because God only knows what could be hiding underneath that tinfoil cover. Admittedly, I was also a bit curious, a trait that never seemed to work in my favor. Carefully pulling the lid away, what did my wondering eyes reveal? A perfectly square block of gummy rice (Caution: rice will jiggle if prodded with chopsticks), cabbage, and a square piece of prefabricated meat. Once again, I had that familiar backing-up feeling somewhere deep in my stomach, a feeling that had dogged me since my arrival in China. As the culinary judge and jury, I dismissed the thought of even tasting the smelly cabbage and the prefab meat square out of hand. This left me with a block of rice. I soldiered forth and plucked some of the starchy goo onto my chopsticks but then returned to it to its rightful place. Once again, what was I thinking? I carefully covered up this delight and proceeded to the nearest trash can. On my way, I could not help but notice how everyone was busy with their chopsticks and eagerly shoveling food into their mouths, complete with looks of sheer delight. I was missing something.

I woke up cramped, disoriented, sweaty, and thirsty. That situation is normal for me, at least in China. I looked out the window and saw what appeared to be a brightly lit tollbooth that resembled something from the Ming dynasty. However, it had neon lights. I must still be dreaming. Are we close to our hotel? I asked the driver. "Yes, yes, hotel." This time he was true to his word as we pulled into the center of a seemingly deserted town; anyone with an ounce of brains was probably asleep in their beds or had left town when the Americans were coming.

Meishan City

We met the local party official responsible for our health and safety at the hotel. It was now close to midnight. We checked in and handed over our passports. The official asked us if we were hungry. "Yes," I replied, "quite hungry for sleep." She laughed politely, covering her mouth, such American silliness, and said, "Very important people waiting for you many hours we go now eat and drink." Holy crap Batman at this hour? Do we make a fuss and create an international incident? We were disheveled, disoriented, and exhausted. However, we all smiled.

A block from the hotel, we were in front of a restaurant, tables, chairs arranged on the sidewalk, candlelight, and food laid out for our much-anticipated arrival. The dinner would happen, even if it meant shaking us awake occasionally. If necessary, CCP slogans would be repeatedly administered until we surrendered and fell in line. We dutifully shook hands as we were introduced to local party officials and a few other stringers associated with this midnight sidewalk dinner event. Smiles all around, it was time for a welcome toast. I knew a toast from the senior official could be extended but could be distilled down to four or five words when translated. Only what we needed to know, of course. As an Imperialist running dog, I'm finding a lot of that goes on in China. Dinner by faint candlelight consisted of choosing from a plate of grilled beef, pork, or tofu, on skewers. These were liberally seasoned with a dry, spicy Sichuan rub guaranteed to raise the dead! I love spicy food, don't get me wrong, but this made my hair stand on end, my heart race, and I broke out in rivulets of sweat. All eyes were on us. "You like, yes?" While gasping for air, I assured everyone that it was delicious. This pale face had no intention of backing down just yet.

In my travels to China, there is one tradition I have come to know quite well. The tradition is that guests are honored first as part of the group by the leader, then individually with "one-on-one" toasts." It can be challenging, especially after the fifth or sixth toast. Our midnight dinner was no exception; one of several hosts would appear at my side with a small bottle of firewater and engage in a short welcome speech which was Chinese to me. Then we would toast. I encourage everyone to try this a few times, especially when they bring out the advanced "white lightning" 106-proof wine, and the shots start. Hang on to your stomach. At home, I keep my gift bottle in my kitchen if I spill some paint. It's remarkably effective.

A BEIJING HOTEL:
INTO THE BELLY OF THE BEAST

When traveling in China, sometimes I feel like banging my head against the wall. That's called Lost in Translation, just like the movie starring Bill Murray on a business trip to Japan. After a while, one's best efforts to reach out and communicate quickly turn into frustration and hopeless despair. Welcome to Asia.

I am different from the careful forward-thinking packer many savvy travelers claim to be. I usually start packing as an afterthought, with just enough time to give myself enough room to wake up in the middle of the night. I typically remember that I need to pack underwear. This time was no different, and why should it be? With barely 48 hrs. before taking off and the joy of fastening my seat belt for fourteen hours of Hell crammed in a crate, I realized my suit needed altering, just a bit, mind you, to match my physique. I shall leave it at that. I thought to myself, no problem because in all of Beijing, there is bound to be someone who can do alterations. It was axiomatic, just like there had to be a laundry service somewhere in greater Beijing. Just a wild guess on my part, you understand.

Once safely installed in my hotel in Beijing, I proceeded downstairs and inquired at the front desk if the hotel had anything remotely like a tailor on staff or at least someone who could do minor alterations for customers in distress. The ladies behind the desk met my question with confused but polite smiles.

"What is a tailor? Please, you write down." The secret word was then fed into an online translation tool, and then oooh, ahhh... smiles were everywhere, heads nodding up and down. It was a teachable moment, to be sure. Of course, now they understood, but then, with more embarrassed smiles, some with hands over their mouths, they said,

"No tailor." "Hotel no tailor, sorry." They were almost savoring the very word for the first time. And I am sure that they were.

I felt that surge of irritation rising in me as if I expected the impossible to happen because I said so. I said,

"Do you mean to tell me that in all of Beijing, there is not one GD tailor who can do alterations on a man's business suit?"

Smiles all around and more heads nodding. More smiles. I decided to pull the trump card, the card I didn't want to play but felt I had to; there was no other choice.

I said, "Well, I'm very disappointed." Emphasis was placed on 'very disappointed.' I paused for effect, then went in for the kill.

"I must speak with your big boss now."

The effect was electric. In a millisecond, this humble American had turned into kryptonite. I was swiftly ushered out of the lobby as if I were a political dissenter who must be kept out of sight and was led through a labyrinth of hallways, one elevator after the next, going through one set of doors and then yet another, deeper and deeper into the belly of the beast. I had no breadcrumbs with me. I was indeed screwed in every sense of the word. My guide led me through a narrow hallway which, at the time, was lined on both sides with hotel staff of various stripes. These included cooks, cleaners, busboys, housemaids, intelligence operatives, and God knows what else. I had made it in time for the AM briefing session/pep talk on handling stupid foreigners and their silly demands. As I passed through the line, I could not help but seize the moment nodding curtly to one side then the other and occasionally grunting a hello in Mandarin as if I were the "big boss" on a site inspection and there would be Hell to pay for any wrinkle sheets. Heads nodded up and down, and shy smiles were offered to the big hotel boss, who was indeed here to kick someone's ass back into ancient times. I must admit, I enjoyed the moment.

We made a sharp left through swinging double doors, and I found myself the lone round-eye in a cavernous laundry room.

Super-sized laundry carts were everywhere, piled high with sheets and towels and sweaty attendants running this way and that, filling gargantuan washing machines. It reminded me of stoking coal fires in the belly of a massive steamship or perhaps someone shoveling coal as in the movie "The Sand Pebbles." Moments later, the doors swung open, and the big man entered. Impeccably dressed. He listened carefully to my tale of woe and confirmed in English that the hotel could not help me. I countered, "You mean to tell me that in all of Beijing ...." He looked at me, one eyebrow raised, incredulous that any human soul, let along an American, would dare to even question him. Finally, he replied, "I have a friend who does tailor work for a few embassies here in Beijing; I will ask him. So, what is your room number?" I was dismissed and swiftly escorted out through one door, then another; multiple hallways and elevators finally resurfaced for air in the hotel lobby where my long journey had begun.

Later that evening, there was a discrete knock at my door. It was the big guy himself, the one I thought would stuff me in one of the industrial dryers and let me cook for a while. This time he arrived without a tie and looking quite the dapper gentleman and man about town. "Hi there, Mr. Richard; my name is "Bruce," and I manage all housekeeping matters for the hotel." We first exchanged mobile phone numbers to ease the transfer of the highly prized goods masquerading as a suit. I called his number, and he seemed delighted that my number had appeared. However, it didn't work in reverse—a Chinese puzzle.

My pants were now in the possession of a mysterious tailor and one who supposedly plied his trade to the U.S. Embassy if I was to believe my new friend "Bruce." Maybe he planted listening devices in the suits of embassy personnel across Beijing?

Not a far-fetched scenario for a good CCP member in this city of Heavenly Tranquility. I wondered if certain people in Virginia had thought about it. I was told my tailoring would be returned the evening before the event. I was satisfied. By ten that evening, my good friend told me the tailor had been in a car accident and would arrive late for the fitting. "So sorry, Mr. Richard." Eleven o'clock came, and a knock on the door; it was the mysterious tailor escorted by a housekeeper. All went well, and may I add that I have never experienced a more perfect tailoring job in my life. I felt almost ambassadorial. I left a note for Bruce at the front desk with a small token of appreciation included. The letter and the appreciation intact found their way back into my room. No sooner had I opened the message than a knock at my door. So many Oriental coincidences or perhaps it's CCTV (I would suggest it stands for Chinese Communist Television.) Who's watching who? I thanked Bruce profusely, but he thanked me for the opportunity to provide excellent service. Hello America, what's missing on our side? I looped my comments back to the corporate office in Virginia. "Bruce" and I plan on having a drink next time I am in Beijing.

THE HOUSE AT TWELVE GINGER LANE

Legation Street, circa 1920s-1930s

I was directed, or wordlessly pointed, in the general direction of a massive public square. "Down this road?" I asked again, raising my voice in English, this time to be better understood. The old man nodded and smiled toothlessly, again pointing as if he knew my destination.

I walked down the well-worn, winding, narrow street once known as Ginger Lane and now little more than an odd historical curiosity, a side road that somehow had managed to fend off the demolition derby of the people's relentless march towards progress in this, the City of Heavenly Tranquility. Was I hoping to find by chance some overlooked bit of memorabilia, forgotten from the days of the Legation Quarter with its history of diplomacy and intrigue, missions jostling for power and advantage, scandals, grand dining, and white mischief from days gone by? Perhaps I would even find that quaint old-world restaurant tucked away at number twelve; surely, it still served a heady variety of exotic Asian-European dishes. With its ceiling fans straining mightily to move the still air, the charming hostess with a warm and inviting smile would beckon me to a corner table with a small delicate vase of flowers on a freshly starched tablecloth. As evening approached, I watched from my table as the lanterns, one by one, would slowly illuminate Ginger Lane. From somewhere in the distance, I heard the faint scratchy sound of music straining from an old gramophone. And a woman's laughter, clear at first then slowly drifting away into the night.

An Unresolved Murder in Peking

The Fox Tower at *Dongbianmen*

It is said that the Fox Tower has been haunted from the moment it was founded in 1564. I felt uneasy being there; that's all I can say. The name comes from local lore that claims deadly fox spirits inhabited the tower. Interesting, but what really picked my interest was not so much the fox spirits running about. Instead, I was intrigued by an account of a grisly murder of an adopted daughter of a retired British diplomat on the eve of the

Japanese invasion in 1937. The historic fortification is said to be haunted by the ghostly specter of a gruesome murder. In his 2011 book, Midnight in Peking, Paul French retraces the victim's last steps in Peking. An unresolved murder today. It is a fascinating piece of work.

TAIWAN

With the communist victory in the Chinese civil war in 1949, the Nationalist-controlled Republic of China government and 2 million Nationalists fled to Taiwan. They continued to claim to be the legitimate government of mainland China and Taiwan based on a 1947 Constitution.

I ARRIVE IN TAIPEI.
A CAPITAL CITY

$\mathcal{N}$o sooner had I landed at Taiwan Taoyuan International Airport than the humidity hit me over the head with the force of a frying pan. It would have been perfect, and I would not have been the least surprised had I seen a crate of chickens pass me by on the conveyor belt squawking for Purdue to save them from their sure death. On board, heading to Taipei, the flight attendants musically addressed you. It wasn't long before yours truly was mimicking their special tone. I found I enjoyed doing it.

One lady even turned around and nodded her head. It must have been something I said that sounded real. Go figure. Sometimes, I impress myself.

I was battling yet another change in time zones. I decided to leave my watch on US time early and figure out the local time on the ground. While my long wool overcoat was perfect in Beijing and Seoul. Today, in Taipai, just holding my coat felt like I was selling wool carpets on some dusty corner in beautiful downtown Karachi. I started thinking about my last Asia trip during the monsoon season in India and Vietnam. It felt the same in Taiwan, with humidity levels nearing 80%.

Waiting for my suitcase after several trips to Asia, the scene at baggage claim looked all too familiar. It's a noisy gaggle of sing-song voices, people grabbing their suitcases, sometimes just taped-up boxes with" beaucoup" string for added security. It all came back to me now. Was I in Deli, Hanoi, Saigon, or Seoul? Honestly, this part of the world was becoming one big, sweaty blur for me.

Once you've exited the baggage claim nightmare, you run into your usual row of people waiting for their weary travelers, armed with their signs for a hotel, perhaps some company big wig, or even a lost round eye like me who only wants to get the hell out of Dodge City. The signs are not always in English, so it pays to be sharp, or God knows where you will end up. I did a second pass, and sure enough, my full passport name was written on a piece of flimsy cardboard. It was held up by a grinning ol' Mister Grey Hair with an all but toothless mouth. He ushered me out and pointed for me to stay put in the sub-tropical humid island weather that is Taiwan.

I stood still and watched him walk away. This was going to be fun. As soon as the inevitable drops of sweat started accumulating on my back, I was drenched. Finally, Mister Grey Hair pulled up in a black Mercedes SL. I got in and settled down. It was heavenly cool inside. He pointed to a row of cold bottled water. Heaven sent. I felt like Lawrence of Arabia returning from the desert, parched with an incredibly mighty thirst. Taiwan and Seoul airports have something in common. You need another day to get from the airport to the city center. From Inchon International, for example, you can catch an express bus for $10 that will get you to downtown Seoul in an hour and a half, or you can take the non-express and eventually arrive. I hit Seoul just in time for Friday evening rush hour, and by the time I arrived, another day had passed (almost). Taipei gives you the same memorable experience. A drink or two on my arrival helped set me straight.

Just a few words worth mentioning about my hotel.

In Taipei, I stayed at the Grand Forward Hotel. I'm not sure of its meaning. I keep calling it the Great Leap Forward Hotel. I found that people were not as amused when I added a little *Mao-naise* humor. Behind the desk, two lovely young ladies greeted me, one in Chinese and the other in English, with two or three words in English. I could have replied in Mandarin, with my fluency of five words, but in doing so, ensuring I didn't unintentionally slander their heritage like the good American that I am. So, I replied in French, which worked out just as well, and we hobbled along in pidgin English and French with smiles all around. Comparatively speaking, this hotel was a different beast. The Great Leap Forward Hotel is indeed elegant, the rooms appropriately spacious, and more than enough room in a bathroom with a large walk-in shower the size of a city block and a separate giant tub that looked like you could easily do laps. We would see about that later.

I took a quick look at my surroundings, several blocks one-way, several blocks the other. It helps me get an initial feel for my little world for the next few days. I saw a combination of Seoul's downtown madness with a dash of Hanoi and Saigon thrown in for good measure. You had sidewalk vendors selling something mysterious on the grill; I had no intention of investigating further.

One thing about traffic. As armies of motor scooters vied for traffic space with trucks, cars, and buses, there was no mad honking of horns. This made places like Delhi, Hanoi, and Saigon truly honking madhouses. But here in Taipei, I hear honking in a regular fashion, one that says, "Move, or you will be run over." It is a distinction with a difference. I considered trying to find an interesting-looking little restaurant where I could enjoy the sights and sounds of this vibrant part of downtown Taipei. But it was not to be unless I was interested in sitting at a table built for midgets and having a choice of three questionable dishes. I was just not in the mood and returned somewhat disillusioned and had dinner at the hot pot restaurant in the hotel—simple concept, your choice of spicy oil or not, with a selection of thinly sliced beef. You could get some sushi-mi or troll the food bar for something else to bathe in hot oil. It's not bad once you get used to it, and yes, the floating tofu cubes do add some taste. Another mug of Taiwan Beer, and then I was off to my room.

Tomorrow I will meet my distributor and his team at their office. There will likely be more exciting slices of life ahead of me.

To give you a peek ahead, my driver gets lost in Taipei on the way to my meeting. Not exactly a good start to my visit. I eat world-famous dumplings in a twenty-second-century shopping mall. They were spectacular and worth noting. I had tea at

General and Madame Chiang Kai-shek's home. Both failed to show. I was a little upset. Later, I fight off hordes of mainland Chinese pouring out of tourist buses, all wanting to view ancient (BC) Chinese Jade. Finally, I witnessed the invasion of the Panda Bears. I almost forgot to mention, over dinner, a couple of small but noticeable seismic disturbances. What's to worry about? Have another beer.

A Day in Taipei: From Dumplings to Tea with Madame Chiang Kai-shek

THE APPOINTMENT

I broke protocol today; some would say I ignored the "Opsec" or operational security protocol and paid for it. You see when I go out to meet one of my business representatives in whatever country, I try to arrange a car at my hotel. It saves time and avoids confusion; I can enjoy less stress in the process. This time I waved away those cares and said, of course, I would take a cab. The hotel dutifully called me a cab, and I made sure I wrote out the address, which took several sentences. I'm always leery of any street address that includes far too many numbers, such as mine, which had 7 F, No.12, Lane 609, and Section 5. I guess they did not need the "the old oak tree" as an additional marker. All this before having even written down the name of the road. The hotel front desk clerk assured me the driver knew where he was going, "no problem at all." Fine. I've been in some strange places before where one is just a little leery about stepping out of the car.

After veering off the main highway, my driver started making left and right turns through little alleys and reappearing in civilization, only to go through another alley. What bothered me was that he kept looking at the address, and the neighborhood looked more and more challenging. It reminded me of a Nigerian taxi driver I once had who felt that two GPS instruments were needed to ensure he got his passengers to their destination. As luck would have it, two GPS were not enough. The Nigerian got hopelessly lost in a lovely part of Atlanta I did not care to be. Back to my story, finally, my driver stopped, got out, and motioned me to stay in the car. It would have made a perfect spot for a hit right then and there, as I was a sitting duck and fully expecting, at any moment, to be saying hello to an RPG whistling its way through an open window. My driver returned, and we went around the corner, through a parking lot into a small street next to a large building. He got out again and showed his paper to someone who pointed to the next building, and off we went. Finally, we both got out. Where in God's name was I? Was this to be the end of the road for me? I was as far from Kansas as any place. I nervously followed my driver, who inquired with someone yet again about the address. My driver then nodded at me, pointed at a row of elevators, and showed me five fingers, then two fingers. Seventh floor, I got it. I paid him, and we parted ways. Each very happy to be going our separate ways. I made it safe and sound, wearing a suit that looked as if it had never dried out. I only hoped they had air conditioning. I was slowly dying in Taipei's humidity.

LUNCH AT DIN TAI FUNG RESTAURANT

*A*nybody who knows something about dumplings – the art of making them and the enjoyment of eating them – will tell you that when in Taipei, you must make sure you visit

Din Tai Fung. This restaurant is not your cozy place nestled away someplace, with softly dimmed individual lights, quiet conversations and the serene sounds of Asian music in the background. This Asian gem is located on Xinyi Road in New Taipei. My host treated me to a special lunch and assured me I would not be disappointed. I like those culinary setups. I was ready. One gets to the restaurant first by entering a new-age shopping mall with escalators that seem to go into the sky. Every modern brand and breed you can think of in the mall, fashion, gourmet, food, perfume, clothing, and everything smells of money. Lots of money.

Dumpling-making is an art desired by many but mastered by few. Every dumpling pastry is delicately hand-made to measure precisely between 4.8 and 5.2 grams with an exact 6 cm diameter before being stuffed to weigh between 20.8 and 21.2 grams. It's a science and art that's taken very seriously. I let my host lead, and he ordered some spectacular ones. These include soup dumplings, truffle dumplings, and some dumplings happily sitting in wicked 3-alarm chili sauce. By the end of the meal, I was dabbing my head, drenched in perspiration, and feeling damn happy. On our way, we watched the process of dumpling filling live. I asked my host to explain the story behind the various Tom Cruise photos scattered about. Yes, that's right, pics of Tom working the dumpling line. He had been marketing one of his upcoming movies, and like everyone who is anybody, he went to Lin Tai Fung's restaurant.

Tea at the Home of General Chiang Kai-shek

After lunch, I decided that a nap back at the hotel would be a splendid idea. However, my host kindly informed me that he had the rest of the afternoon free and would be my guide around Taipei. How could I refuse such an offer? Our first stop was the home of General and Madame Chiang Kai-shek. It is a quiet and reflective place with beautifully tended gardens and serene hidden ponds to contemplate. However, on this day, the Chinese Communist finally invaded the island but without firing a shot. They had a secret weapon unknown even to our intelligence services. My host, apparently not a fan of the mainland and its revisionist history, was quick with his smirks and comments. Busloads, one after the other, belched out eager tourists from the mainland all dying for a peek at the home of the man who "stole" China's treasures and therefore must remain vilified because, well because Mao said so. Hard to refute that line of thinking.

All in all, from what I could tell based on my extensive interior decoration skills, which were nothing, the residence was tastefully done with a mixture of Chinese and European pieces. The general's bed was on display. My host whispered that the General slept alone because he snored. A tidbit of information, I would wager, is not found in most history books. Readers should add this to their cocktail tidbits of information no one care's about. We saw the formal dining room with seating for a dozen or so, the family's more relaxed living spaces, the library with a quaint television set from a bygone era, a lot of Madame's paintings, as well as some interesting black and white photographs including an original photo of the General with FDR and Churchill at the Cairo Conference in 1943. Madame was also present.

The National Palace Museum, Complete with an Expert in Chinese Jade

We drove to the National Palace Museum. I was told it was a must-see, especially for a man like me surely of refined taste. He is a clever one! The museum has the most extensive collection of Chinese artifacts and artwork representing 8000 years of Chinese history. My host reminded me that with Mao attempted to destroy all elements of Chinese culture, erase the past and create a more proletarian society. General Chiang Kai-shek countered by emptying as many museums as possible and then making his way to Taiwan – then known as Formosa. As a result, mainland Chinese are curious about their heritage. Some say these visitors come to see what was stolen. More reason, I would argue, for Communist China to be concerned about Taiwan's misinterpretation of Mao's revisionist history and its alignment with pro-Democracy countries. My host introduced me to a friend who works at the museum as a researcher specializing in the study of ancient Chinese jade, his passion. He explained the art and meaning of a piece of jade dating back to 500 BC. Let me assure you we were not alone, as hordes of tourists from the mainland were everywhere, pushing and shoving to see anything. Was this the beginning of the cultural takeover of Taiwan? I began to feel my host's pain.

As we left the museum, it was late afternoon. The humidity subsided somewhat, reminding me of a pleasant early summer evening. Warm but comfortable. Looking up at the hills around us, you could see the tall spindly palm trees shooting up from the dense, almost jungle-like vegetation. I felt an MGM moment coming on and called for my First Sergeant (John Wayne) to get a squad and recon those hills.

LIBERTY SQUARE AND PANDA-MONIUM

The last stop on my seemingly never-ending tour of Taipei was Liberty Square, sometimes known as Freedom Square. It is a grandiose public plaza covering over 240,000 square meters. At the east end of Liberty Square stands the National Chiang Kai-shek Memorial Hall. The square is surrounded by the National

Concert Hall on the north and the National Theater on the south. It is an impressive piece of real estate, and I suspect it is Taipei's answer to Beijing's Tiananmen Square. I thought seeing over a thousand lifelike pandas on display was most unusual. It was indeed pandemonium. I never did find out about the truth behind the panda story.

It was evening, and the lights came on as we left Liberty Square. We stopped for dinner at a "Western" style restaurant near my hotel. It seems it's a Chinese custom to wait until the end when your Western customer has been softened up with kind words and food only then to bring up serious business matters. And so we did, over a couple of cold Taiwan beers and steaks; only briefly were we interrupted by several tremors. The rattling and the shaking of glasses and plates were unnerving.

My host did not miss a beat. "Oh, it's quite all right. We have those all the time."

SOUTH KOREA

SEOUL CITY NIGHTS

*T*here is a sing-song aspect in people's voices that I've noticed. It started first in Taipai, then in Seoul, where one is greeted almost musically, and the tune sounds like "ding-dong the witch is dead." Linguistically, I think it's not totally a Korean thing, at least according to my host in Seoul. A strong Japanese connection with

Korea has left a lasting influence on this country. Koreans would like to forget that connection, as the Japanese were vicious masters during World War II. It's not something that can be easily overlooked, and every so often an article appears in the press on this very issue.

I looked out my hotel room window in Seoul onto an eight-lane city street flanked by office buildings and shopping malls. I wondered if I was in downtown Chicago or Arlington, Virginia. I have a commanding view from the fifteenth floor of downtown Seoul, South Korea. The air is terrible today. My business contact advised me to stay inside. A grayish-brown haze that has blown in over the Yellow Sea, courtesy of China. I had a few lousy air pollution days while in Beijing, and it has followed me to Seoul. I am indeed a most lucky one.

My hotel is in the heart of the intersection of Insanity and Madness. This is all fine to a certain extent if you want to run out and shop for imitation everything or an abundance of useless trinkets to take home to family and friends, only to find out people in the US already have these gems. If your idea of a meal is eating at a cozy Asian restaurant shoulder to shoulder with the locals or perhaps chomping down on a burger or enjoying Colonel Sanders fried chicken, then this is your place. For example, my room had everything I needed and enough space and convenience to satisfy the maximum needs of cost-efficient business travelers/tourists. It's a French chain of hotels, and I know from experience that the French can build some highly "efficient" hotels that many would consider downright spartan. You see the same efficient hotels in France built for economy-minded French families on their way to spend August at the beach. Unpleasant and uncomfortable comes readily to mind; however, the chain always had rather good food, at least in France. Mess with that, and you can expect riots the next day. More garbage on the streets and cars burning; who needs more of that? Back to my hotel in Seoul. Then there was my bathroom. As you entered, you turned on the bathroom light, and the toilet console (yes, that's right) lit up like something from the starship Enterprise. I felt I needed a user's manual as some things looked rather dangerous, let alone highly unusual. Enough said but worthy of note. Only the French would insist on having that!

Two blocks from my hotel is the *Myeong*-dong or Main Street. It is a pedestrian mall with narrow side streets jutting out to the right and left. The mall is a maze of stores selling everything from cheap junk to name brands with questionable pedigrees. It also has sidewalk vendors selling beef on a stick, fruit, and other unrecognizable food items. You can stop at a Starbucks, slowly and patiently wind your way to the counter and order a latte for around 5000 dongs or just under $5.00. Step outside past the bubbling bathtub in front of Le French bath products, and you pass a Burger King with its window advertising extolling the virtues of a super-sized burger and the promise of a heavenly meal and who knows what else. I seemed to have found the epicenter of what I left behind in America.

Everything you may have seen in those useless catalogs determined to clog your mailbox at home can be found here. The crowd is overwhelmingly young, pushy, and dressed in every conceivable combination – think Backstreet Boys meet Cindy Lauper, and you begin to get the idea. Young men wearing lime green, vinyl-pointed tennis shoes, and multi-colored spiked hair and women in various gaudy micro or spandex outfits and often seen teetering in mile-high sneaker heels, all of which leave little to the imagination. That's an excellent point of departure to let your imagination run wild. From every storefront comes the techno music's thumping, head-splitting sounds. The crowd is deep and slow-moving as you wind your way up the *Myeong-dong*. In many ways, it reminded me, but only somewhat, of Barcelona's Las Ramblas but on steroids.

At last, I met my contact, but only after taking three wrong turns off the main street and down various bubble gum alleys. We met at an authentic Korean restaurant. I've plenty of experience with authentic Chinese restaurants in Beijing and was prepared for more unrecognizable food rapidly being laid out on a giant lazy susan. And me with my chopsticks attempting, often unsuccessfully, to stab with the faint hope of landing a thick multicolored piece of something. But this was not to be the case. I was presented with a steaming bowl containing rice, beef, vegetables, hot sauce, etc. Following the lead of my host, I carefully used my stainless-steel chopsticks to mix and remix the contents, thus ensuring the contents would be steaming hot. I was instructed not to touch the bowl unless I wanted to risk third-degree burns. Along with the chopsticks came a third utensil, a chopstick with a small spoon. Now, why can't the Chinese do something like that? Just asking. Along with the meal came cold tea and a local chocolate-flavored brew with a kick to it. Certainly nothing wrong with that!

Much to my surprise, I found that my host was quite knowledgeable on political geography and history relating to the Korean peninsula. He was also quite well-versed in global affairs. We had a pleasant and instructive (for me, at least) dinner, and I came away with a better appreciation of the meaning of "who rules the Korean peninsula rules Asia." Not to be outdone, this lovely

Korean restaurant even had entertainment with a young lady in traditional costume playing the *Ajaeng,* an instrument that has seven strings of different thicknesses. The performer used a stick made of a peeled forsythia branch with pine resin. That is something that should rank up there in meaningless cocktail factoid chatter. Yes, you can thank me later. We left the restaurant and had coffee at Starbucks – how homey! I asked him about Korean history, politics, and language, and he was willing to continue. Overall, it was a lovely way to enjoy a Seoul city night.

How do you say Goodbye in Korean?

I'm despondent at the thought of leaving my newfound Korean friend. I would not be surprised if he showed up at our office one of these days. He has a son in Minnesota and another in

New York, working on a degree from Columbia. After a night of traditional Korean food, I took the day off and did nothing, which suited me just fine. Come Monday; I was on deck in my suit, tie, and briefcase—time to work. We made our way through town in his silver Acura with an Asian voice chirping each time he took a right or left turn. In front of the office building, an underling awaited my arrival. He promptly opened my (door, took my briefcase to the office, and deposited it in the conference room. His job was done. The second in command then came in and bowed (Japanese influence, once again). We each presented our business cards (holding them with both hands as is the custom). We studied each business card carefully before putting it away (as is the custom). We waited for the big guy, my host, to join us. I would be giving a PowerPoint presentation almost identical to our company president's presentation in Beijing. Ten underlings in dark suits entered the room, each bowing before sitting down with their notebooks and pens ready. Additional chairs were brought and arranged; we were prepared. I was introduced, and all ten underlings rose at attention from their chairs in respect (notice any similarities with Japanese customs yet?) Instruct us, oh wise master of the universe, so that we may learn from you and one day sell you everything you don't need. And indeed, I did. They left quickly and as quietly as they arrived, all bowed as they went out. It was a most unusual experience.

My Korean host invited me to lunch, including his trusty sidekick, the marketing director, and smooth-faced, ever-smiling older gentlemen. Very nice. Having had an official Korean dinner the evening before, he assured me we were going to a Western restaurant. I found the restaurant to be entirely European and less

American. I handled that with great appreciation. Korean steak or Western steak? I chose the former. Ever the culinary diplomat. It was a delicious meal from the "*amuse-bouche*" for starters down to the dainty little desert that one might have confused with a smudge on the plate. I could learn something here. Maybe.

Having said goodbye to my host's trusty sidekick of 20 years, we cruised for a quick spin around Seoul. We drove up into the hills above Seoul that once had been fortified to fend off Genghis Khan and his crew, who seemed to enjoy burning, pillaging, and raping their way through Asia. The Japanese arrived much later to finish what Genghis started. From our vantage point, we had an excellent, though slightly smoggy (courtesy of the PRC, so I was told) of Seoul city. I asked my host just how far we were from the D.M.Z. I didn't play basketball and doubted my presence would have been welcomed when crossing the border. We were less than a half-hour from the madness of the North Korean regime and the little tyrant with the bad haircut. My host decided it was time to do a U-turn and picked a lone gated driveway to maneuver. Two seconds later, an unsmiling South Korean military guard appeared at the gate with a nasty-looking machine gun pointed toward the passenger side. Apparently, some years ago, a team of thirty North Korean special operations soldiers crossed the border and passed through these very same hills. Their sole purpose was to assassinate the country's President. All but three were killed. Those who escaped, I suspect, were probably received as something less than heroes.

It was a great afternoon, and I was delighted to have met my Korean host. I am sure we will see each other again soon.

ISTANBUL, TURKEY

From Europe to Asia in Twenty Minutes

"If the earth were a single state, Istanbul would be its capital."
—Napoleon Bonaparte

"The great trains are going out all over Europe, one by one, but still, three times a week, the Orient Express thunders superbly over the 1,400 miles of glittering steel track between Istanbul and Paris."
—Ian Fleming

odern Turkey was founded in 1923 from the remnants of the defeated Ottoman Empire by national hero Mustafa Kemal. He was later honored with the title Ataturk or "Father of the Turks."

From Taksim Square station, our point of departure, the funicular swiftly and smoothly shuttled its passengers down to Istanbul's waterfront in minutes. There, just a few feet away, the commuter ferry to *Uskudar,* on the Asian side, was ready to push off. With a ticket in hand and a prayer, I jumped aboard along with a few other stragglers who had shared with me that moment of insanity, deciding whether or not to take the great leap forward. We slowly pulled away from the European continent, leaving behind a dramatic and colorful waterfront of palaces and mosques. We started to cross the choppy Bosphorus Straits that divide this intriguing city in half. Crossing the Straits seemed a bit like a game of chicken. One commuter ferry dodging the other ones. The traffic was brisk on this relatively short, twenty-minute commuter ride from the European to the Asian side.

Other commercial boats were plying the waters of the Bosphorus, but when you had the massive tankers going through to the Straits, you realized how just how small you were. These tankers were heading to or from the Black Sea, towards Eastern Europe, Russia, and beyond. Ever curious, I had yet to learn where my other passengers might be going or who they might be. They could have been tourists, government officials, secret agents, or men and women just anxious to get home for dinner. I admit, I did at least half expect to meet Graham Greene or Ian Fleming on an undercover assignment for his Majesty's Secret Service. Let's be honest; Istanbul has been a Mecca for spies for many years. Did such uber writers of excellent spy fiction, like Ian Fleming and John Le Carre, Eric Ambler, and of course, Graham Greene, just happen to find themselves at some point in Istanbul? Not likely.

As a point of interest, it's also well known that noted spymaster Kim Philby, a British MI6 operative and Russian double agent, frequented the city, undoubtedly meeting his agents or perhaps briefing his Russian masters. In his usual off-handed matter, my father once told me that he had met Philby. Nothing further was offered, and no questions needed to be asked because no answers would be forthcoming. I was left to wonder and decipher the same way I had with other tidbits of information. It has been a lifelong quest to learn more, to try and put the pieces together, to create some picture, a mosaic of his professional life and, to a certain extent, even his early professional life—case in point, Philby. This discussion will occur again later in this book. There are other pieces that I have pursued until the trail runs cold. Granted, I get a little obsessive and have been known to spend hours combing the internet looking for a piece of information to add to the puzzle.

Please bear with me now as I go down the rabbit hole for just a moment. When would my father have known Kim Philby? There were several avenues that I chased down, perhaps from his days in London during the war, which would make sense. My father was initially in London until just after Normandy, and then he moved with his detachment to Paris. He was with OSS-X2, the counterespionage unit established by "Wild Bill" Donovan to provide a secure means of interfacing with their British colleagues and assess sensitive German intelligence coming from Ultra and the whiz kids at Bletchley Park. At that time, our man in question, Kim Philby, was already a senior officer in the British

Intelligence Service, known as MI6, and likely already serving two masters—it is a fascinating back story on the Soviet recruitment of Philby and his colleagues at Cambridge. In retrospect, Philby, who was part of the Cambridge Five, was an indictment of the British upper-class system. How could Philby possibly be spying for the Soviets; he was, after all, "one of us." It was inconceivable and therefore not possible. For the British secret service, it proved to be a disastrous blind spot.

Ironically, in 1944, Kim Philby was appointed by MI6 as co-ordinator of a newly created special anti-Soviet intelligence operation—an ironic twist of the fox guarding the hen house. The second option in my search was that perhaps my father had met Philby in Paris just after the war. The situation then was fluid, with old allies becoming adversaries and vice versa. Everything was changing. Maybe Philby had already appeared on OSS-X2's radar, however the British did not reveal their suspicions about Philby until well after the war. As a person of interest, they could easily have crossed paths at some official function in Paris. A third option to consider, perhaps my father met Philby while briefly detailed in Germany, stationed just outside Berlin. As one person told me, "We (your father and I) watched the Russians shelling Berlin. We knew the war was over." Lastly, perhaps the two met while in Washington, D.C., though the dates don't necessarily align with my father's side of the equation. One thing is for sure, in this sort of exercise, the more one goes deeper into the intelligence rabbit hole looking for clues, the more opaque, complex, confusing, and unclear things become. I suspect that is all by design. And all the more challenging.

As we passed near Maiden's Tower, I was reminded of a pleasant fellow in Turkish history known as Ibrahim the Mad, who, at the ripe old age of 24, on learning that another man had seduced a member of his happy harem, proceeded to have all 280 of his concubines nicely sewn up in sacks and delivered to the murky depths of the Bosphorus. Why was he called "mad"? I will let you work on that one.

On the ferry boat to *Uskudar* on the Asian side, one passenger looked vaguely Russian. Bad habit of mine, I suppose. Was it his waxen face or the scar on his cheek that made him look unusually threatening? There would be no secret *rendez-vous* for me, no appointments at an unassuming address somewhere high in the hills, no chalk marks on a park bench confirming a meeting, and no seamless handoff from a passing asset. At least not this time. I had a far simpler agenda than playing cat and mouse with foreign agents on the Asian side of the city. I looked forward to a quiet, pleasant dinner meeting with an old friend.

Maiden's Tower (Turkish: *Kız Kulesi*)

However, the Turkish *Millî İstihbarat Teşkilatı* (MIT), the Turkish National Intelligence Organization, thought otherwise. I was invited to their headquarters on the Asian side. Having carefully studied my thick, well-worn passport with visa stamps worldwide, the interrogating officer noted, "It seems you have presented quite a compelling, almost convincing story for being in Istanbul. Congratulations. Indeed, Mr. Richard, perhaps this is also an excellent cover story, yes? So, let me ask you again, why are you really in Istanbul, and what is the nature of your business?"

I probably would have replied, "No need for you to pick up that well-worn telephone book. I am prepared to share all my transnational culinary secrets. And I wish you good luck in following them!"

On the Asian side, I hailed a taxi and gave the driver the address adding:" Hurry, man, I am being followed, lose that car" (no, not really). The restaurant is strategically situated on a hillside overlooking the Straits with an expansive view of Istanbul's European side. The restaurant was named *Balıkçı,* which means fisherman in Turkish. Once inside, there was no mistake whatsoever. The walls, decorated with wood wall panels, created a cozy atmosphere. There was a liberal assortment of photos and paintings adorning the walls, many by famous Turkish artists. The Fisherman prides itself on delicious fresh fish and seafood varieties and a creative cuisine staff. Since 1920 the restaurant has been in the same spot serving delicious food with great mastery.

A few words about my charming Turkish host. A well-educated, trilingual gentleman. We spoke in English, while sometimes we slipped easily into French. I noticed that when he says something in Turkish, it's never a short sentence; instead, it sounded like a machine gun at Gallipoli, rattling off words in a seemingly never-ending sentence. He would pause, breathe, squeeze the verbal trigger, and enter the next series. I was chagrined to learn that his lovely wife was unavailable for the evening. She is quite the beauty if I may say so.

My host insisted we start with an octopus salad which he said was unsurpassed anywhere. How could I say no? I recalled, all too well, the fate of the last octopus. Having witnessed its previous last few dying moments on the edge of the Aegean Sea. Keep that story in mind when we head south towards the Aegean. In Turkey, it's safe to say that no matter what meal you enjoy, there will be a sampling of *'zeytinyağli'* or vegetables cooked in olive oil and served cold. They are delicious, and the olive oil is fantastic. We raised our glasses with the traditional Turkish 'raki' or the Lion's Milk, an anisette-flavored liquor, like your Greek ouzo or a French pastis. It will give you a top-notch quality headache the following day; by then it's too late to check if you still have your wallet. One should enjoy it carefully. I may have had more than one or two celebratory toasts, but I'm unsure just how many. After three, I no longer count.

The menu was a cornucopia of fresh fish from Turbot and Red Mullet to Grouper and Lobster in season. Everything looked delicious. What caught my eye was lobster in green curry sauce. That hit my sweet spot for sure. It was more than delicious, and I made a point of wrestling the recipe loose from the kitchen without creating a diplomatic incident. By then, I was comfortably *raki*'ed, and my host called a cab so that I would return to my hotel via the Bosphorus Bridge (officially the 15 July Martyrs Bridge) crossing rather than risk losing his U.S. customer to the inky dark waters of the Bosphorus. Bad for business.

MIXING IT UP ON ISTANBUL'S ISTIKLAL STREET

By Zumrasha – Own work, Public Domain

I don't think you can find a busier, crazier, more colorful pedestrian free-for-all than Istiklal Street in Istanbul in the heart of the Beyoglu district. You don't stroll on this street; instead, you move defensively and hopefully in a forward direction, conscious of the shifting waves of humanity crisscrossing from one side to another and the occasional vintage tram that persistently moves up and down the street, slicing the crowd in half. The street is to Istanbul, the way the Champs-Elysée is to Paris, and Broadway is to New York City. Istiklal is an incredibly bustling thoroughfare approximately 1.5 kilometers long and chock full of shops, cafes, legendary pastry shops (to die for), bars, restaurants, and fast-food joints such as Burger King, KFC, the Hard Rock Café are there amid stately 19th-century architecture.

The street stretches from Taksim Square to just past Galatasaray Square on the north side of the Bosporus. It's estimated that nearly 3 million people visit Istiklal each weekend day. I cannot confirm that, but I can tell you that the street was bustling on a weekday. There was an explosion in 2016, the day before I strolled down the road. It happened on a side street just off Istiklal, the very side street where I had been. The newspapers attributed the incident to the Islamic State. It's a packed street and offers self-proclaimed terrorist groups an opportunity to inflict maximum damage with relative ease. Six years later, in November 2022, another bomb exploded on Istiklal Street, killing six people, and injuring 81 people. The bombing was attributed to a Kurdish insurgency, long a thorn in the side of the Turkish Government. In any event, it was too close for comfort, even in daylight. The street: It's where life happens.

For my last evening in Istanbul, my customer graciously invited me for drinks at his apartment in Istanbul. This is his home when he is not with his family in Izmir or on the coast. It offers a sweeping view of Istanbul and the Bosporus. It was a most memorable photogenic opportunity.

My last evening in Istanbul with a view overlooking the Bosphorus

A Fishing Village in Southern Turkey

Do not be fooled into thinking I am again rattling around in the South of France. Admittedly, from my photo, it could be a fishing village south, perhaps Antibes. Good guess, and while I like the idea, you are dead wrong.

Allow me, dear readers, to recount for you a snippet of a story about my stay in a small, picturesque Turkish fishing village that hugs the Aegean Sea and is just a few miles from Izmir, a bustling city if there ever was one, with a beautiful bazaar deep in the old town and just ready to swallow you up.

I had finally arrived, but only after my driver had made several wrong turns and reached my destination under cover of darkness with my bags, passport, and a terrible thirst for a strong drink. Arriving somewhat incognito was good because I would have attracted more than your average share of curiosity and questions about there being an American in town. I wanted neither. The sleepy night desk clerk quietly observed my efforts as I struggled toward him with my oversized suitcase in one hand. I also carried a carry-on and computer briefcase in the other. I reached the desk, looked at him, smiled, and rang the bell. Two could play this game. He looked back at me and uttered the universal word understood by all weary travelers: "Passport." It was an excellent beginning. He then made enough gestures for me to realize that my signature was desired on a document written entirely in Turkish. I signed and, in doing so, prayed that I did not just agree to be taken to Istanbul and thrown into a Turkish prison. Let's say the movie Midnight Express kept running through my head. Grumpy, the night clerk, reviewed my passport with much interest. I felt like I was crossing the Czech border at midnight in some God-awful Cold War movie where everything is grainy, in black and white, usually raining, and generally uncomfortable. At that moment, I felt I could still run from the Turkish secret police, who had already been called. The night clerk nodded his approval but only after carefully inspecting my passport from cover to cover, upside down.

I was handed the key to room 205, and up I went, climbing the narrow, winding stairs, panting, and tugging at my suitcase and balancing the computer bag, one damned step at a time. The room was furnished in the early 1950s Turkish beach house style, as I had no idea what Turkish beach house styles might look like. But I was probably close. Beach houses are beach houses. The paint chipped here and there. The bathroom looked challenging, and the shower was foreboding. The bed had a noticeable starboard tilt to it. Only one plug was in evidence, and even though it was hanging out from the wall, that would be for my iPhone and computer source, even if it meant the power surge might blow up the hotel. Opening my porch door, I stepped out into the inky darkness of night. I could immediately smell the Aegean. Somewhere in the distance appeared faint hints of light dotting the horizon. I could hear the sailboat lanyards' occasional clanging against the masts. The air had that strong fish smell. Somewhere along the waterfront, I listened to the faint sound of music and the mumbling of lyrics I could not even understand.

The following morning after remembering where I was, I stepped out onto the porch to try and get a sense of my bearings. It was a bright and clear morning. There was no evidence of any fishing fleet though I vaguely recalled hearing trawlers firing up their engines as they prepared to head off for a day of fishing in the clear waters of the Aegean. I saw some unknown land masses far into the distance and a single trawler working the seas back and forth close to shore.

I was hungry and decided I would play at a "guess that land mass" later. Downstairs I was greeted by a lovely young lady who pointed the way to a door. "Breakfast, yes?" she said in broken British English. The breakfast was a buffet of strange-looking foods, some I thought had no business seeing the light of day. I reviewed the dozen or so dishes looking for something I might recognize. I went for some salty goat cheese, olives, tomatoes, hard-boiled eggs, and something resembling a bagel. I mastered the multiple-options coffee machine and was ready for a feast on the porch overlooking the water. The same friendly lady who politely steered me to breakfast came by and inquired, in her best English, if my accommodations were satisfactory. She followed up with:

"You are from Washington, yes?" That was close enough for government work, and I nodded as I worked through my boiled egg. Not to be deterred in her mission, she continued:

"We have guest also from Washington; she is a big basketball player."

I could not recall the names of any basketball player, let alone an alleged female superstar in Washington, DC. Maybe I simply could not recall, or maybe I just didn't care. I think I knew the answer.

I feigned complete and utter surprise at this marvelous news. I told her that I sincerely hoped I would meet this famous basketball star. How exciting! I was tingling in anticipation.

She smiled, I smiled, and we smiled and nodded at each other. More juice, please?

I thought about the day's agenda. There was lunch. Maybe I could walk the village from end to end. Dinner would be a business meeting with my client driving in from Izmir and bringing customers who had flown in from Ankara. He told me the name of the restaurant where we would have dinner. I planned to check it out during my village visit. Maybe things could get interesting in this quaint town.

An Aegean Lunch

I know some people who love to spout off, "Oh, you could tell the fish was so fresh, we were in heaven," blah blah. You know the kind I'm referring to, the humdrum conversationalists, and as soon as they open their mouths, you start yawning. That happens to me more often these days. It's not their fault, of course. I just get irritated more often than before. Anyway, dear readers, let me tell you about the true definition of fresh fish.

During my lunch, I sat in a quaint little restaurant, like so many others, fronting the Aegean, and you could see the fishing boats and the men setting up their nets for the next day. There was much laughing but also a relaxed sense of serious purpose. It was lovely and quiet.

A loudspeaker's call to prayer shattered a short-lived quiet, and Iman's pre-recorded voice carried across the quiet fishing village. I had never seen so many people appear out of nowhere on their way to the mosque. The call to prayer wrenched me back into reality and even made me spill my wine. That was the injustice of it all. I can assure you that I learned from the episode and was ready for the next call to prayer. I held on to my wine with a near-death grip. Some things are like religion to me.

I watched a fisherman climb onto the rocks accompanied by several cats who were clearly onto his game. The man pulled something from his bucket that was still moving and attached one end of it to a rope. Now this is where things got weird. After systematically beating the poor tentacled creature, he stopped long enough to wash it in the clear Aegean water. He then resumed methodically swinging the creature from the sea, hammering it against the rocks. I called the restaurant proprietor/waiter over to my table. His English vocabulary equaled my Turkish, so we were good to go.

I asked him in English what was that strange Turkish ritual under my nose. He nodded and asked, "More wine, yes?" I was not getting through and felt like saying, "Who or what is getting the crap kicked out of them over on the rocks? Instead, I did what any intelligent foreigner might do and spoke louder so that he could better understand me. I motioned, like a complete idiot, towards the rocks and looked at him quizzically (or perhaps I feigned a dramatic look of horror.) He smiled at me all the while probably thinking: Could you be any more stupid, Mr. Hot Shot Americano? Instead, he pointed with a gnarly finger, the size of a carrot, at the menu; then, I had an epiphany. The octopus was being tenderized to death, and the poisons literally beaten out of him. This quaint and charming practice, I suspect, is not reported on at any great lengths, perhaps because some animal rights activist would then have an urgent need to scream and demand justice. And that won't do.

Things had returned to normal. No calls to worship, at least for the moment, no more beating sea creatures, and the fisherman seemed to have wandered off somewhere. I was the only soul in the restaurant, savoring a local white wine and maneuvering through the menu selections. I realized dinner would be an event but I had time to kill. That meant eating, drinking, and whatever else I could do to avoid trouble. Trouble finds me. I know this to be true. A short while later, the bottle of wine hovering close to empty, the owner reappeared with a basket full of fried, breaded calamari. I thought about the creature's fate and what I had witnessed. Was I going to drop the dime to the UN High Commission? I shrugged and tasted one. The gates of Heaven open for me because that's where I thought I had arrived. Nowhere on earth exists something as delicious. Period! I ordered another bottle of nicely chilled white wine and sat us straight because this was a serious culinary treat. Dinner was a while away. I ordered another basket.

CASABLANCA, MOROCCO

"Tonight, he'll be at Rick's. Everybody comes to Rick's."
From the movie, "Casablanca"

CASABLANCA AND THE MISSING LETTERS OF TRANSIT

Photo by Smartyzs - *wikipedia.*
org/w/index.php?curid=62232963

*H*aving been to a variety of souks and markets of various sorts from Cairo to Izmir and a few places in between, I feel I can go out on a limb and say that some are very good, colorful, and entertaining and, in most cases, you still have your wallet when you emerge into the unforgiving Moroccan sunlight. There are no longer instances of the French police blowing their whistle and chasing some poor creature through the side streets or hesitantly into the souks. Or better yet (if I must go here), no German police chasing after someone who might be holding letters of transit. Here in Casablanca, life is cheap. I was in Casablanca for a short business stay and planning on visiting my customer at his office in the *France Ville* section of Casablanca. I was also anxious to peek at a well-known market, the Central Market or *Marché Central.* Just a quick note on the history of this market because I am quirky that way. The Central Market was completed in 1917, the year my father was born, and a year before the end of WWI. There I am trying to connect almost everything I can to one historical event or another.

Case in point. The cashier at my local go-to-market does not understand my constant use of historical references, despite my attempt to interest her. She routinely ignores me when I tell her about the irony of my total grocery bill coming out precisely to the very dates of the Battle of Waterloo or the Battle of Trafalgar or the end of the war in the Pacific or whatever. "Don't you find that interesting? Again, she looks bored. I slid my card through the machine, and it wordlessly flashed a critical message: "Press Yes if you would like to donate to the starving children of East Wangu?"

Allow me to take you on a short literary exit ramp. On arriving in Casablanca, I felt like I had been there before for some reason. I felt transported back to my days in the Heart of Darkness, known as the Congo. Kinshasa and Casa (as the locals call it here) suffer from a long-standing post-colonial fever. You can build modern structures, and repave roads, especially those used by visitors, and giving your airport a glitzy look will also help. Still, the fact remains that you are traveling in a post-colonial city. You can rest assured that all the bad habits of past colonial masters have not been forgotten. They have been passed down from one ruler to the next, and if anything, they have been honed to near perfection.

THE "ROCKEFELLER" BAR

*A*cross from my hotel was a little cosmopolitan joint called the "Rockefeller" on the Boulevard D'Anfa. I was too curious not to go in. Once I parted the beaded curtain and entered the darkened room, I found myself in a charming period cafe/bar with music from another era. I conversed in French with the beautiful young lady working behind the bar. I suspect she ignored that I was speaking French because she assumed I was French. Not the first time. Later, learning I was an American, chastised me for knowing any Arabic. I told her I was fluent in three words. That didn't help. She pouted and returned to washing bar glasses. I was thinking about saying, "My nickname is Rick; maybe you don't remember me; I used to own a café here in town."

Then, the owner, the very "Dapper Dan" of Casa himself, sporting a white evening jacket and black bow tie, made a dramatic appearance walking down the ornate circular stairway. He was a nice fellow, Arab, but quite charming, even though he was originally from Cleveland. He had a habit, I noticed, of getting things done with a mere look, a nod of his head, or a finger casually pointed. Staff responded swiftly, murmuring, "Yes, *effendi.*" This was getting interesting. A mother-daughter couple came in. They spoke French, so I engaged the daughter, and we spoke in French. I learned she and her mother were originally from Toulouse but had lived in Pointe-Noir, Congo (as in Brazzaville) for some time. We talked about Africa, what I missed or longed for from my days in the Congo, and what she missed about civilization.

I asked her: "Who are you really, and what were you before? What did you do?" She smiled, a gentle, understanding smile, the way one might smile at someone who had lost their way in time.

What other characters might arrive next? Would we sing the Marseillaise next? Would there be an arrest here and someone brutally escorted out by two thugs to a black Citroen idling curbside? Was there an issue with forged passports or a passing exchange of uncut diamonds? Had I somehow, inadvertently, slipped into a time warp?

Returning to my market day in Casa, I casually strolled from one stall to another, listening to merchants plying their trade, when suddenly I had an epiphany – perhaps it was the North African heat, I don't know.

THE FRENCH FOREIGN LEGION, "LA LÉGION"

I was thinking seriously about food, more than I usually do, shall we say? Prolonged exposure to the sun will do strange things to men. Just ask *Beau Geste*. I suppose I'm doing a *pied-noir* thing as I recently ran across some interesting French North African cuisine. I could hardly cook alone, so I decided to share a meal with those brave enough to embark with me on my cooking and literary adventures.

As with much of my writing, there is often a recipe behind it. Some recipes are tied to my childhood – *ma jeunesse*, my youth growing up in Paris; others originate from those beautiful vacations at the old family home in Brittany where my mother and *Simone,* our wonderful housekeeper and famous cook, would put meals on the table that rival some of the well-known restaurants in Paris. On that point, there was no doubt. Other recipes I have collected from my global travels, be they in the Congo, India, or elsewhere. I have had the good fortune to have run into interesting characters, including my most colorful friend, Luc, who swears he was with the French Foreign Legion and did his five-year *service militaire* and saw more than he wanted to see. Luc has four fingers on his left hand, and the missing one has never been fully explained to my satisfaction or perhaps my dark curiosity.

I gave Luc the name of *Beau Geste* as I could see him manning the parapets of Fort *Zinderneuf* and squinting out towards the desert, scanning the dunes, waiting for the next Bedouin attack. Perhaps I would throw in Gary Cooper for good measure. How often had Luc shown me how to cut a person's throat neatly and swiftly? I have always thought that he must have spent too much time lurking about in the *Casbah* or perhaps out and about somewhere in the *bled*, a term he used quite often which meant the desert and a word that was invented by the French which derived from the Arabic phrase *baladi* (land).

In any event, Luc traveled to interesting places worldwide on exciting assignments. I leave it at that, or I fear Luc will want to set the record straight with me and in a personal manner. I want to live a little longer if possible, because paraphrasing a line from Casablanca, "It's the romantic in me."

The dish I have included in the recipe section of this book is a Moroccan chicken dish very much like the one Luc, a self-styled *cordon bleu* cooks in his spare time, had served me. In Tangier, it was the food market where Luc first tasted this succulent dish. Readers familiar with Southern France will have undoubtedly tasted something like this, which would make sense. Luc served it up with plenty of chilled white wine and a bottle or two of Rose to be on the safe side. *Shukran,* my friend and *Bon appétit.*

CAIRO, EGYPT

"Put an Egyptian in the driver's seat, and he shows all the calm and consideration of a hooded swordsman delivering Islamic justice."
—Tony Horwitz

Giza

Welcome to Cairo

How does one begin to talk about Cairo, the city of a thousand minarets, let alone do it justice? I would argue that Cairo is the very definition of a vibrant, exciting, noble city at the center of this country's political and cultural life. You can't discuss Cairo without referencing Giza and the incredible pyramids. Egypt, Cairo, the Nile, Giza defy any smug, post-colonial understanding or attempt at some pseudo-intellectual framework. One stands before the pyramids in absolute awe, realizing how little we know or will ever understand.

Yes, Cairo is an Arab city plagued with traffic congestion; let me better describe it as crippling traffic jams and roads and highways with enough potholes to swallow your car up. I mean that in every sense of the word. For example, when my customer was driving me from the airport to my hotel, he hit a massive pothole, I mean a pothole from Hell. It was bone-jarring, and I felt the shocks would surely come through the floor. It readjusted my spine. He laughed and replied in Arabic; I said, "My friend, I bet that by the time you take us back to the airport, you will have hit at least five large potholes." He laughed until it happened again, and I grinned and said, "That's two!" He muttered something in Arabic, something about a thousand camels. Not sure.

Arriving at Cairo International Airport is much like visiting other airports in developing countries worldwide. Inside the airports are all the services a weary traveler would need to face the world outside the front doors. Relatively efficient passport control is always welcomed and certainly not expected. Long lines for everything. With the outside within reach, one's luggage is X-rayed again. On leaving the airport, you congratulate yourself (let's be honest) on still having your passport and wallet and that your suitcase arrived in one piece. You are greeted by a mass of humanity, the smells, the air, the heat, the humidity, the traffic, and the incessant honking of everything mechanized. Cairo welcomes you in its embrace.

Ramadan Ceremonies

In the event that you arrive in Cairo during Ramadan, having miscalculated your arrival time, and believe your life is over, have no fear. Muslims believe that Ramadan is when the first verses of the holy book Quran were revealed to the Prophet Muhammad more than 1,400 years ago. Cheer-up! There is good news. Given that you are your customer's guest (as in my case), Ramadan in Cairo can truly be an experience if you want to get closer to the local culture and see how the people live their lives. For many, I imagine, that thought is too frightening to contemplate. Better to stay in the hotel, eat in, and not go out. Even then, too many "different" people are in the hotel lounge. Cairo is nothing like back home in LaGrange, Wisconsin! Old story, I know, but I repeat it for emphasis.

"In my dream, behold, I was standing on the bank of the river Nile"
Genesis 41:17

My customer very kindly invited me to join his family for a Ramadan dinner boat cruise on the Nile or the Sea of Egypt. I was interested in being on the Nile; this river has been here for thousands of years. With any luck, Pharaoh's daughters would come down to bathe at the Nile. Understandably, I wanted to avoid stumbling over a basket hidden somewhere in the reeds and containing a wee bambino—all the makings of a ancient political mess.

While on board our Nile River cruise, an ample buffet fit for an army was laid out with every conceivable variety of breakfast, lunch, and dinner dishes. It was not yet sunset, and the Iman had not declared it so. Muslim fast as one of the Five Pillars of Islam, an obligatory act of worship. One second after sunset and the authoritative call of the Iman, the buffet table was attacked by adults and children, all placing more food on their plates than I thought possible. How many hours until sunrise? How many cigarettes could one possibly smoke between sunset to sunrise? I suspect quite a lot. But two at a time was it possible? Yes. After the feeding frenzy and given the late hour, there was still time on the clock for an early, pre-sunrise breakfast. Shall we say 3 AM at our house? Lovely.

Is that your belly dancing?

My customer insisted I stay for the show, but I wondered if I was just to cover for him. He grinned and said I should be ready to dance. Right. We were handed brochures with marketing photos of the belly dancer and information about her affiliation. Egyptian-style Raqs Sharqi is danced in boats on the Nile, in hotels, and at expensive weddings. The belly dancer shared the traditional arts with well-choreographed, sensual movements, twirling, spinning, gyrating hips, and brightly beaded skirts to captivating Egyptian music. Because Egyptian law forbids showing the stomach, even when wearing a two-piece costume set, belly dancers in Egypt must cover their torso with a stocking type of material. It was a dizzying, captivating show. I felt like I should be wearing a Fez but in a smoky back room somewhere, deep in Cairo's Casbah. I was momentarily lost in time and remembered that I still needed to obtain Rommel's Panzer Army troop movements and get them to Monty's British Eight Army. I was told my contact was the belly dancer. Of course.

We enjoyed the remaining moments of the evening, everyone now on the top deck, as we slowly made our way up the Nile to our destination in Giza—a truly enjoyable and special evening of Ramadan with our guest and his family.

LOST IN OLD CAIRO, THE GREAT SOUK AL-KHAN EL KHALILI

I suggest visiting the souk in old Cairo if you want to lose someone. I don't want to frighten future tourists who might read this and say, "I just knew it wasn't safe to travel to one of those crazy bazaars." I would advise that should you go, you do so with a local or, even better, with a tour guide and follow him closely as he snakes through the back alleys of the souk. Soon you will be hopelessly confused as to your whereabouts. Job well done! You then follow your guide once more down another alley only to find yourself where you started your adventure in the first place. What a clever trick!

There are so many things to see in the souk; you feel closer to the real Cairo than your conversations with the one Egyptian hotel employee who speaks "little engleesh" and has a brother in Baltimore. In the souk, a guide will help determine the price reasonableness for that small rug or the colorful hanging lamp, the miniature pyramid paperweights, busts of pharaohs, official scrolls with "real" hieroglyphics as seen only on Etsy, perhaps that scarf or a trinket for Aunt Jude as a Christmas present. After all, these are merchants, traders, if you will, not suckers, though they recognize the difference when they see a tourist coming. Postscript: Forget the toilets. They reminded me of the ones in the souk in old Izmir. For a travel veteran like me, that's saying a lot and perhaps some good advice to heed.

The Pyramids and the
Call of the Desert

"Lawrence, only two kinds of creatures get fun in the desert:
Bedouins and gods, and you're neither. Take it from me; for
ordinary men, it's a burning fiery furnace."
Mr. Dryden, in *Lawrence of Arabia*.

I had the morning free, so I decided to see the pyramids
at Giza. I was accompanied by my customer and a trusty
guide he had selected. This guide knew his stuff and had even been
part of a tour guide team on a former President and Mrs. Clinton visit.
We had used him the day before to guide us through the souk. While
getting ready, a television news bulletin announced that a busload of
Australian tourists on their way to the pyramids had set off a roadside
IED. The bus was out of commission naturally, but the tourists were
all safe and sound but some were in shock. Did I feel lucky that morning? Would I go or stay and cower in my hotel? How many lives does a
cat have again? I thought about the Istanbul explosion, which I missed
by a day or so, and now the IED. That made it two so far. I gave
the operation my green light. We were traveling in my customer's car,
which looked like it belonged in Cairo as it had all the beat-up mark-
ings of a local car. Unless the IED were in a pothole, we would be fine.

The desert tells a different story every time one
ventures on it – Robert Edison Fulton, Jr.

The Giza Desert may not look that unforgiving, but before you act on your Lawrence of Arabia fantasy, you should think twice about your safety and hire a guide. Uniting all the Arabs may sound like a lofty goal, as it did to Lawrence. However, let's leave it as a goal, *inshallah*! God willing. If you remember, take a ten-minute drive to the Mosque-Madrasa of Sultan Hassan. You will find it a powerful and moving visit.

Leaving Cairo

We hit the fifth gigantic pothole on our way to the airport. My customer was unhappy, perhaps not for hitting the pothole but because he lost the bet. He said something in Arabic, and I said goodbye in English. I thanked him for his time and for the kindness of his lovely wife and children, who were delightful.

BEIRUT, LEBANON

"Nothing is very constant in Beirut. Beirut is a city to be loved and hated a thousand times daily. Every day. It is exhausting, but it is also beautiful."
—Nasri Atallah

Hezbollah at the
Gates of Beirut

I must admit that it felt strange to arrive in Beirut. My knowledge of political history told me things remained unsettled in Lebanon. This was even more clear when, upon leaving the airport, my customer informed me that we were now passing through Hezbollah-controlled territory. I inquired if this was the same Hezbollah that had ruthlessly killed so many people and shot rockets into Israel for good measure. My customer nodded. Yes, the very same. Still, he reminded me, that as a proxy for Iran, things would remain quiet until urged by the Iranian Mullahs into aggressive action, then rockets would fly again from positions well hidden, most likely in the Beqaa Valley. I recalled recent reports that Israel had threatened to deliver a few missiles to hit Rafic Hariri International Airport because, not surprisingly, they accused Iran of using that venue to smuggle small components for drones and precision-guided missiles. For a moment, I wondered how the Iranians would activate sleeper cells. Perhaps they were waiting for a coded message from the Mullahs to the Imans at a specific call to prayer. It was safe to assume there were viable cells and arms caches throughout Beirut.

Beirut is always prone to violence, rocket attacks, or bomb explosions. I recalled, some fifteen years ago or more, just before the Israeli-Lebanon war, that inquiries were made if our firm, where I was working then, could exfiltrate a U.S. businessman stuck in Beirut. No one had that capability or knew anyone who might. I made discrete inquiries to someone I knew in South Africa, but only through introductions, who would have the right experience. He indicated that what I had suggested was possible and confirmed to me, in the early hours of the next morning, that if he received the green light, our customer's only escape route would be the road from Beirut to Damascus, arguably not the safest route, and at some point, most likely, they would cross into Israel. The stranded businessman eventually decided, or was advised to stay put and not leave Beirut. For whatever reason.

Back to my reality, I noted that the small yellow flags with the Hezbollah logo flew everywhere in an apparent show of support for the home team. All quite different, almost surreal.

That evening, my customer and his wife took me to a lovely restaurant by way of a long, winding, scenic seaside route. The restaurant seemed almost empty; there may have been one another person there. No business tonight. Tomorrow, we would our start our business discussion a fresh. On the way home to my hotel, I was treated to a beautiful Beirut view know as Pigeons' Rock (also known as the *Rock of Raouché,*) a truly stunning set of rock formations that welcome all to Beirut. These two massive formations stand as sentinels to the city. Given that it was late evening, I was surprised by the crowds walking along the promenade and enjoying the evening. It felt like a holiday crowd.

Beirut stands in stark contrast to Cairo, where I had just been. Granted, Beirut has had its share of civil wars, and yes, bullet holes can still be found here and there though most have been removed, some remain as a reminder. There seemed to be a sense that the best move in Beirut is to enjoy today for all it's worth. Another conflict could be just around the corner.

Downtown Beirut seemed elegant today. The French influence, stores, and restaurants have remained. While Cairo was chaotic and dusty, and the traffic was close to God awful, perhaps a complete mess. Don't get me wrong; I love the contrast. I recalled my brother telling me about Beirut when he was here as a young banker in the mid-1970s. Then, I imagine, Beirut must have been at the very height of elegance. It was the Paris of the Middle East. How a fifteen-year civil war can change things so quickly, so dramatically, is undeniable, yet Beirut's inhabitants continue their daily lives. There is no other option.

View towards the Bekaa Valley taken from the Chouf Mountains. To
the East is the Syrian border, and to the South is the Israeli border.

Excursion High in the Chouf Mountains

The following day, our customer drove us high up into the Chouf mountains (in Arabic, *Jabal ash-Shouf*) for some great sightseeing. Chouf is the heartland of the Druze community and their well-known leader, the Progressive Socialist Party leader, Walid Jumblatt. For our customers, it is their home country. The mountains, high above Beirut, were, in many parts, covered with snow even in late spring. There we were in two black Land Rovers speeding through quaint Christian or Druze towns one after the other. My customers feared not. They were on their home turf, their territory, they were safe. Less so for strangers, who were more likely to be seen as intruders. We stopped first to see the legendary cedar of Lebanon, the oldest recorded tree in human history, having first been mentioned some 4,500 years ago and making it older than me. Our next stop was in *Beiteddine,* the name of a village and a truly magnificent palace complex. The palace was the former stronghold of the 18th-century governor Emir Bashir. It was an impressive visit. We then drove further up the mountain until we reached a plateau. You could see the expansive Beqaa (or Bekka) Valley from that vantage point and yes, also uncomfortably close to the ledge. The valley is a strategic region and a key area of operations for Hezbollah. It uses the valley to smuggle weapons and other supplies from Syria into Lebanon and train its fighters.

In 2033, Hezbollah continues to publicly demonstrate its troop strength and taunt Israel and the IDF. It makes for a dangerous game, to be sure. At some point in the Beqaa Valley, along the cease-fire line, it's only a few hundred yards dividing Israel to the south from Syria to the northeast. Looking out across the valley, you can better understand the strategic value of the Beqaa Valley and how Hezbollah, at the direction of its Iranian masters, could strike at the heart of Israel, almost with near impunity, from their carefully concealed locations. For now, one can assume that a strike by Hezbollah against Israel will not likely happen unless and until they are given a firm green light from Iran. It remains a war of nerves, where Hezbollah continues to test Israel's limits. Hezbollah recently fired a rocket into a Jewish border settlement. These types of micro-escalations can only go one way from there. The government of Israel and the IDF must decide how far they will be pushed, taunted, before striking back. All of this has yet to be played out.

The takeaway here is that it's imperative to remember that Hezbollah, a Shia Islamist political and militant group, has an undeniably strong political and military presence in Lebanon. It also has a known record of operating in the Bekaa Valley. The hope of a country finally at peace with a governing coalition reflecting all political parties in Lebanon remains a distant hope at best.

A Family-style Lunch

Before leaving Beirut, our customer invited us to lunch with his family and office staff. How wonderful and honored we felt. So many delicious Lebanese dishes were laid out. Truly a feast.

DUBAI, UNITED ARAB EMIRATES

"Dubai will never settle for anything less than first place" – HH Sheikh Mohammed bin Rashid Al Maktoum.

Dubai is the capital of the Emirates of Dubai and the most populous of the 7 Emirates in the UAE. Dubai is a global transport hub. It also has oil, financial services, real estate, and some goodies that round out the riches that make this a shimmering city on a hill.

I've been to Dubai at least a half dozen times, but explaining Dubai is easier said than done. I have long thought Dubai suffers from an inferiority complex and an expensive one at that. This manifests itself most clearly in a quote from HH Mohammed bin Rashid Al Maktoum wherein he states that Dubai will never settle for anything less than first place. I have every reason to believe that is Dubai's philosophy.

I have wondered if Dubai has a heart and soul like many big cities we know like London, Paris, Madrid, Chicago, and New York. All have a heartbeat, whether commercial, cultural, or historical. They have souls. Dubai is different. It's over the top, consistently, and I would suggest, deliberately. One could say that if Dubai does not have a soul, Dubai will find and buy the very best "soul" that money can buy. Sounds absurd, I know; until you go to Dubai, then you understand better. Remember, "Dubai will never settle for anything less than first place."

My parents would have called Dubai "*nouveau riche*." It's as if a rich little kid wanted to show everyone everything he could buy with all the accumulated money. Sometimes, Dubai makes it a point of being "in your face." Will the world take us with greater seriousness if we have the biggest this or that than anyone in the world? Dubai chases the finest of everything while enjoying its balmy over 100-degree temperature. Yes, Dubai is in the desert, but would you like to snow ski? No problem, we have that, complete, I might add, with a fake fireplace to convince you that you are somewhere in the Swiss Alps. Do you need a spectacular room at stratospheric heights with outlandish accommodations, complete with a famous French chef, who just flew in for you? I think we have that. Is that for this evening? And so, it goes on. Ignore the massive traffic congestion in the morning and evening rush hours. I suspect there will soon be a high-speed elevated super rail, but that may be too banal. Think bigger and bolder, don't worry about the cost. Do you wish to see an entire community carved out of the ocean and designed as a palm tree with a tunnel underneath? Yes, we have that. But wait, we have so much more.

A dust storm day: The sands of the desert are never far away.

DEMOCRATIC REPUBLIC OF CONGO

INTO THE HEART OF DARKNESS

"Sadness flies on the winds of the morning, and
out of the heart of darkness comes the light"
– *Heart of Darkness* by Joseph Conrad

Leaving Paris, France

*T*hen it happened, just like that. One day in April, my father announced that it was time to bid our teachers and our schoolmate's farewell. We were USA-bound for a few months before leaving for some strange, unheard-of place in Africa called the Democratic Republic of Congo.

I wondered if in my excitement at the thought of thumbing my nose at the school authorities or sticking my tongue at my nemesis, my teacher, the embodiment of all that I knew was evil, I might be jumping from the frying pan into the fire.

I don't recall if I quietly screamed with joy at the prospect of cutting my ties with Hell or recoiled at the prospect of saying goodbye to Madame X, the torturer of the 16e *arrondissement*, the same one with the deadly right hand that never missed and always landing on the chubby cheeks of this American.

It was an enjoyable ride to school; as usual, we were late. However, this time I did not care, and I made it to my classroom and stood outside waiting for permission to speak to my teacher as instructed or else. Yes, or else what, send me home? Would they take me on another walking tour from classroom to classroom, while the Assistant Superintendent holding one of my ears firmly in his hand? Much to the other children's amusement, of course, and much to my humiliation? Perhaps one more slap to set me straight so I would finally learn something? The French state does not suffer mediocre students. With as much solemnity as I could muster without smiling, I told my teacher that I was leaving and would return home to the United States, that's right, the big PX in the sky, land of double-bubble gum, Coca-Cola, and supersized candy bars. I would never return. My teacher scornfully looked me up and down as if I were damaged goods, after all perhaps best suited for the United States. The French educational system would be better off. Then in a sweet and sympathetic gesture, she swatted my right arm, telling me to "get my hands out of my pockets; it's rude." I thanked her and told her I appreciated my farewell party, the witch!

I don't recall any packing fuss or movers coming to carry out furniture; instead, it was like any other day. I remember having a small Pan Am duffel bag and my Pan Am wings, which I wore; one never knew when the pilot would need my assistance, so I had to be ready. We closed the door to the apartment, fully furnished, untouched, dishes clean, and beds all made. And we left.

Once stateside, my brothers and I were farmed out to two sets of relatives. I went to Pittsburg, and my brothers went to Connecticut. This was a chance for me to get to know my wonderful cousins. While my mother stayed with her mother in Philadelphia, my father was dispatched to Washington for training before leaving to for the Congo. It was a strange but also wonderful summer at the same time. By August, we were all united at my grandmother's beach cottage in Cape May.

Cape May Taxi to Idlewild Airport

Dr. Livingston, the irony of it all is quite extraordinary.

After spending my time running around the streets of Paris, as I have written in my first book, *A Long Look Back,* we found ourselves eighteen hours later on a Pam Am flight from New York, granted with a brief stopover at the Jersey shore and eventually arriving in Leopoldville. My mother, four siblings, and I along with multiple suitcases all squeezed into an old taxi station wagon.

Traveling from Cape May, NJ, to New York then to the Congo, we must have made quite a sight. It was a journey I would never forget.

I had no idea what to expect when I arrived in the Congo. I had read the authoritative version of the Congo's history as told by *Hergé* via *Tintin, au Congo*. I would quickly discover that the reality of the Congo was far removed from the 1930s book version. Though not that far.

Our Pan Am flight left from Idlewild Airport, later renamed JFK International, shortly after. The Pan Am Clipper jet made multiple stops along the West African coast. Our first stop was in Dakar, and we got our first taste of Africa, the smells, the incredible heat, and the humidity. We all disembarked with my mother leading the way and shepherding five children, including my youngest sister, then only an infant, to the transit terminal. Later, we would then reembark and settle in again. The process would repeat itself each time we landed in Monrovia, Accra, and Lagos. Finally, we landed in the dead of night at *N'djili* airport. Welcome to the Democratic Republic of Congo. For me, it had arrived at the very end of the world. I felt as if I had taken a wrong turn and somehow dropped off the face of the planet. No one would ever find us. *Tintin* had been right all along; this was dangerous territory, and soon we would join him in a large stew pot. In retrospect, my mother was a saint for undertaking such a voyage. She ensured we all arrived safely and that no one was left behind at some spot along the West African coast. This expedition into the vast Heart of Darkness was, for her, likely about as far as anything she was used to; either her days as a WAC in World War II, her life in Paris, or for that matter, in Philadelphia, comfortably surrounded by her family, her brothers, and sisters that she missed dearly.

N'djili airport, Leopoldville, DRC 1960

Arrival at *N'djili* Airport, Leopoldville

In retrospect, clearing customs must have been like a scene from Dante's Inferno. A journey through Hell. For me, it was something I had never witnessed before. Yet, in hindsight, as an adult and having experienced the joys of landing in places like Cairo, Delhi, Beirut, Jakarta, Hanoi, and more than a few others, they all seemed to have certain unsettling similarities. The scene was all too familiar. We arrived in 1963 when the Congo, with its capital city, Leopoldville (Leo to local hands), had just recently gained its independence from Belgium, its former colonial masters. Under the benevolent mantle of promoting Christianity and trade in Africa, Belgium systematically and ruthlessly had exploited the Congo's riches, including rubber and minerals. As such, the young country, now newly independent, was still fragile, unsettled, politically divided, corrupt in many places, trigger-happy to a large extent, and quite vulnerable to increased foreign influence. The new country could hardly have anticipated that it would soon be caught in a global power squeeze play.

We were in the arrival/customs area, patiently waiting our turn as we slowly inched forward. Passengers from other flights were also there, gathered under one roof. There were French, Germans, Belgians, Americans, Indians, and more. It was a veritable UN, and many likely were associated with it.

Young soldiers were on patrol, holding their machine guns. I am convinced they would have easily opened fire at the first sign of any disturbance. I would add also that it would not have come as a surprise to have found out their magazines were empty. You just never knew. The customs inspectors, dressed in military uniforms, barked at unlucky passengers demanding they open their suitcases to find something they liked. The inspector might add it to their growing collection of seized "illegal" goods, American cigarettes, Cognac, perfume, and other tradeable goods, all safely under the table. You could acquiesce to the inspector's wishes or try to bribe him with a wad of Congolese or U.S. dollar bills. If the inspector saw a good deal, he might let you pass or call his supervisor and rat you out for attempted bribery of a Congolese official. If that happened, well let's not ponder such an unpleasant scenario.

By this time, it was late in the evening and hot, and the smell was beyond belief. It was a combination of body odor, rotten fruit, and jet fuel fumes. They had forgotten to install air conditioning, but that would be at least twenty years later. I was tired and growing more than just a little uncomfortable with my surroundings. We finally passed through customs and saw our father amidst the crowd of Congolese who were waving and yelling at friends and family. He could not have stood out more had he been holding a sign saying, "I am an American." It was a thankful site to behold. My father had arrived in-country a few months earlier for business and had arranged for a house in the suburbs, not too far from the missionary school.

We took the long ride to our new home in the dark of night, finally reaching our destination for the next five years. Had I known that then, I would have staged a protest.

Post Colonial Leopoldville

The Belgian Congo was a Belgian colony from 1908 until independence in 1960. The city of Leopoldville was established as a trading post by Henry Morton Stanley in 1881 in honor of King

Leopold of the Belgians, who controlled the Congo Free State. Since independence from Belgium, the Congo has endured war, instability, division, and deprivation.

In Leopoldville, later known as Kinshasa, a story circulated in the ex-pat community about a German Ambassador who decided to go waterskiing, fell off his skis, disappeared underwater, and never re-surfaced. It's not one of those myths you want to challenge and prove wrong. Falling into the Congo River could significantly reduce your lifespan as it was a well-known fact that the Nile crocodile species inhabited those waters and had an average size of 15 feet or more and weighs at least 500 pounds. It would make mincemeat out of an average human. One bite, and you become two. It's that simple, the magic of it all. Occasionally, I would read about adventurers who believed they had the "right stuff" and could tackle the river. The story usually has a tragic ending. I recall one story where the guide, who was in his kayak, tipped over and under. The kayak came up empty. Truly the beast lives up to its name as the "man-eater of the Congo."

The Congo's temperature is furnace-like on a good day, and the humidity wraps, unforgivingly, around you like an old carpet. It can be suffocating, and if you are not careful, the combination of the heat and the humidity could point you to an early grave as it has too many and will continue to do so. A comforting thought, indeed.

In this part of the world, they speak Belgian French, which is still the official language. In addition, they speak many other dialects, including *Lingala*, a colorful-sounding river dialect of clicks and unusual-sounding words of which yours truly, still remembers but a handful after more years than I care to imagine.

My linguistic abilities with the local language made the men grin, then return to picking their teeth, and the mamas, wrapped in colorful fabric, howl with laughter. I still have high school classmates, many of whom grew up in missionary families and eventually made their lives in the Congo. No need to return home. For what? Their Lingala is as fluent now as it was when we were in high school.

A quick sidebar, under President (General) Mobutu Sese-Seko (Emperor for Life), he renamed the country Zaire, a name derived from a mix of Portuguese and local in-country dialects. Years later, in 1997, under the regime of General Laurent Kabila, the country was renamed again, but this time back to the Democratic Republic of Congo.

I recalled the Congolese army (*L'Armée Nationale Congolaise* (ANC). These young men, mere kids, had suited up for the promise of a meal and a few Congolese Francs each month, if that. They wore helmets that seemed to cover their eyes and fitted out with overly starched uniforms that would have stood by themselves. A quick sidebar, when traveling to and from our home to downtown Leopoldville or to and from the airport, it was not unusual to be stopped by the police and IDs were checked, and occasionally, papers were carefully scrutinized, sometimes upside down, for greater clarity, one can only assume. Most could not read or write a single word but would shoot with little hesitation if the white man foolishly decided to run. It became a dark joke in the ex-pat community.

Another absurdity of Congo life was the clear understanding that if you were ever involved in a traffic accident, or worse, you hit a local, the best strategy was to leave the scene as fast as possible. On seeing you go, there had been instances where Congolese crowds would turn on the car behind the one that left the scene. This happened to one of our good friends who would have been severely injured had an American not arrived in time to rescue him. Our good family friend recalls the incident as if it were yesterday, and he is always thankful for the rescue.

Home Sweet Home

I can recall, as if it were just yesterday, waking up on my first day in Leopoldville, the capital of the Democratic Republic of Congo. I was hungry and went in search for food. In the living room-dining room, all the furniture had been removed, and Albert and Emanuel, our two houseboys, in their work whites, were busily washing and waxing the large green and white tiled floor. They saw me, gave me a big smile, and came over and introduced themselves in French, of course. Albert, the senior houseboy, inquired if "Messe" Richard would like breakfast.

That first day looking out from our back veranda that swept the length of the house, it was clear this was nothing like Paris and the big PX in the sky was far out of reach. Below the veranda was a well-manicured garden with several large Frangipani trees with beautiful fowers that bloomed year-round. Beyond our garden and past a crudely built wooden fence that ran the length of the property were manioc fields. From there, a valley of deep vegetation stretching down into the unknown.

In the evenings, when the heat and humidity hung stubbornly over everything, bats would rush out from under the eaves and up into the sky; lizards would appear along the walls and ceilings, searching for smaller prey, and the monkeys high in the trees would utter an occasional scream from their perch somewhere in the darkness.

Then, you might hear the muffled tom-tom sounds from a little village somewhere in the valley. Of course, my mind would conjure up the worst from all the movies I'd seen or adventure books I'd read. In his best Graham Greene-like manner, my father, with a cigarette dangling from his lips and a scotch in his hand, would tell me, matter-of-factly, "Richard, it seems the natives are restless tonight." I would return to my room feeling less than comforted, lie in bed, and listen to our night watchman playing his thumb piano as he walked the property. My father would return to his scotch and await the arrival of a mysterious midnight courier.

"The monotonous beating of a drum filled the air with muffled shocks and a lingering vibration. A steady droning sound of many men chanting each to himself some weird incantation came out from the black, flat wall of the woods."
– *Heart of Darkness* by Joseph Conrad.

THE CONGO WILL STAY
WITH YOU FOREVER

"We penetrated deeper and deeper into the heart of
darkness" *Heart of Darkness* by Joseph Conrad.

Several years back, when I was living in the Washington DC
area, we had a terrific summer thunderstorm that rattled
your teeth with the ferocity of the thunder. My dog had aban-
doned me long ago because, as a human, I was too stupid not

to hide under the bed. As I listened to Mother Nature doing her thing, my mind raced back, as it frequently did, to those days when we lived in Africa, the heart of darkness, the Congo; we lived in a seemingly never-ending months of torrential rains then to be followed by scorching, hot days. The cycle was unforgiving. During the rainy season, life was dialed to a slot rot. Everything remained damp, and it was a breeding ground for every living creature known to man, both visible and invisible.

Creepy Crawler

One day, I found a nasty red lump on my arm that did not seem to be getting any smaller. The redness was spreading, and the bulge was growing bigger. The situation was handled in a field hospital manner, first by filling the bathroom sink with water as hot as I could tolerate. Then, with my arm submerged, I waited patiently. Sure enough, after a while, with the skin on my arm softening up from the hot water, a worm-like creature crawled out in a cork-screw fashion holding an "I Surrender" sign (not exactly). One of the houseboys washed all our laundry; I believe it was Emanuel. He dutifully ironed each piece, hoping to kill any eggs that might have nested in our clothes. While this was not a full-proof process, it helped keep our bodies free from those large red lumps. Our drinking water was boiled daily and stored in plastic pitchers in an antiquated refrigerator, operating on one leg. Only a fool or a local Congolese would dare drink water from the tap. I can't even begin to list all the diseases in Congo. Still, they ranged from Flu, Ebola (more so in the bush), Hepatitis, Typhoid Fever, Tuberculosis, Tick-borne Encephalitis, and more. There was a good reason why we had submitted to over a dozen shots before our departure to the Congo. I recall we did it in installments over several weeks. It was a sign. I should have packed my bags for anywhere right then and there.

School days in the rainy season were damp from beginning to end. We moved our desks out of Harm's Way if the rain and wind got too intense. Those strong winds had a side benefit. A large mango tree was on the school grounds near one of the teachers' homes. The heavy winds inevitably would blow ripe mangoes to the ground. We scrambled and collected as many as we could. Delicious.

It was just as damp at home, and sitting at the dinner table was unpleasant. In retrospect, I suppose our idea of discomfort paled compared to some of those who worked for us. One day Albert, our head house staff, arrived almost in tears explaining that the monsoon-like rains had washed away his entire house. This was a yearly event. The monsoon rains were like that. Looking back, it's no surprise that I felt right at home when I traveled the world, from India, Vietnam, Indonesia, and elsewhere oftentimes during monsoon season.

Albert lived in what was then called "*la Cité*" at the time, an indigenous city within a city where houses were made mostly of sheets of plastic, some wood, and a piece of corrugated metal sheet for a roof. Cooking and washing were all done outside. A white face was hardly ever seen nor, I suspect, particularly welcomed. Plain and simple. I recall one isolated instance of driving with someone into "*la Cité*," possibly we were bringing something to Albert. During these times of personal crisis, my father would always try to help by providing some extra cash or advancement in wages, and my mother would offer extra food. We did what we could. It was our reality.

Malaria Sunday

It was malaria pill day every Sunday afternoon, after church and lunch. My father dispensed the horse-size tablets, and we dutifully swallowed them. However, one or more of my brothers may have pretended just to defy my father. It had to happen. It was inevitable. First, my father caught malaria. I recall seeing him on the bed in the study as he alternately shifted from shivering cold to burning up. My mother finally called on Dr. William T. Close urging him to admit my father to the hospital, where he has his practice. Inevitably we three house kids would each come down with much milder versions, but complete with the requisite fever, chills, and general discomfort. I should note that Dr. William T. Close, as mentioned above, was a childhood friend of my father in the 1930s when well-heeled Parisian society "summered" at Le Touquet. That factoid was mentioned in my first book, *A Long Look Back: A Sentimental Journey of an American Growing up in France*. I have often wondered how surprised each were (if at all) to find out that their boyhood friend was also in the Congo. Dr. Close was also the personal physician of President Mobutu Sese Soko, then President of the Democratic Republic of the Congo, later known as Zaire. To this day, I find the coincidence of their both being in the Congo at the same time, unusual, to say the least.

An Invitation to a Hanging

On one occasion, our two houseboys, Albert, the senior, and Emanuel, second in command, asked me, in all sincerity, if I would like to go with them to witness a public hanging. During the early Mobutu years, one of his favorite means of consolidating power was to publicly execute his political rivals. There was a certain finality to it all and note of caution to all those with regime change on their minds. Hanging rivals, I think, narrowed down the list of possible candidates. Regime discipline if you will. Most likely, the hanging would have taken place at the central prison of Makala. Even without a hanging, incarceration at Makala prison was a death sentence in of itself. I understand it continues to hold on to its gruesome history of accidental deaths. Thirty or more are "offically" reported dead very year from malnutrition, suffocation, or lack of primary care. I would presume a fair amount of prisoners fall on knives for some strange reason. A charming place then and still is today. I would not be on the lookout for 60 Minutes to do a segment on inmate rights in Makala.

My answer to their kind invitation to a hanging was sincere; however, I thanked them for their consideration.

The following day I asked about the hangings, and they both made gruesome faces and choking noises while twisting their heads back and forth. Lovely, I thought to myself. Now, about breakfast?

Regarding power consolation, Congo-style, I remember hearing about the regime's persuasive squads who would gather up known opposition leaders and introduce them to the gaping mouths of the ever-hungry Nile alligators, who lurked in the Congo River waiting for a meal they knew would eventually come, though likely kicking, and screaming.

After weeks and months of seemingly never-ending rain, it stopped. Finally. Just like that. As if someone had found the spigot and declared, "Oh, that's where it is!" and promptly shut off the water. You woke up in the middle of the night because something had changed. The rain had stopped. It was no longer pounding on the roof. The next morning, the sun shined brightly; it was a beautiful day and the beginning of the dry season. And how dry it would become. After a while, all the moisture had turned into a cloak of humidity, and the unrelenting heat had cooked everything to a dull brown. Bright green leaves and grass turned crispy brown, and people moved slower in the heat. Many of the side roads, which had been little more than muddy rivers, eventually drained, and would dry up leaving deep gullies almost impassable by car.

For the locals, it was business as usual. The dry weather meant we would see the "Mamas" women walking door to door with their huge fruit bowls balanced atop their heads with papayas, mangoes, bananas, coconuts, and more.

We had a dog, a Boxer, named Jeff, who had, shall we say, an "African" problem that we could not resolve. When the "Mamas" came down our street with their giant bowls laden with fruit balanced on their heads, Jeff, as if on cue, took off immediately in their direction. He leapt high over our garden wall, making the *Mama's* scream in absolute terror at the sight of a large Boxer gone airborne. The papayas, bananas, mangoes, and whatever else they carried fell, landing and rolling around in the street. My father would offer a few Zaire banknotes, which worked at first; after enough time, the local *"gendarme"* drove up to our house in his military jeep and informed us that we had two alternatives: Either we relocate Jeff, or the police would return and kill him. Of course, we found a new home for Jeff. Nothing more was said about the incident; from then on, the *"Mamas"* safely resumed their commerce.

A Taste of Congo Politics

AP Photo Simba!

It's almost impossible to write about the Congo and not talk about hard-nosed Congolese politics where only a ruthless, strongman can ever survive. This was the Congo as I knew it.

Shortly after we arrived in 1963, I recall when we would drive downtown, it was not unusual to see a jeep with a white soldier decked out in full camo gear, casually holding a machine gun or standing behind a mounted heavy caliber machine gun. Casual but ever vigilant and ready. He was most likely a mercenary, especially in those early years, and likely from South Africa for Europe. Various Congolese factions hired their own mercenaries, some of whom even worked with the U.N.

The Congo had just gained independence from the Belgians three short years earlier. I think it's safe to say the mood was as relaxed as a trip wire. The country was about to go from much-desired independence to impending domestic chaos. The Belgians had reluctantly given the new Congolese government the keys to the kingdom, but the directions were not included. The thinking ran like this: "You want independence? Then figure out how things run since you want it so much". Before that time, the Belgian administration ensured that no Congolese would ever be in a position of responsibility. Not surprisingly, without a cadre of seasoned bureaucrats, the years following post-independence Congo were characterized by confusion, disorder, and various factional conflict, all wrestling for political control of the newly independent Congo. The US News & World Report, on 8 August 1960, some months after independence, noted the following: "As authority broke down, senior white civil servants who knew how to make the government operate panicked and ran for their lives." The economy collapsed when white business directors, industry managers, and technicians followed suit. There was also panic amongst the ex-pat community, especially the Belgians, as they fled or attempted to flee to save their lives. I recall seeing gruesome pictures of Belgians, bloodied as they attempted to flee Leopoldville for the airport and the next Sabena flight out of the country. As the government and country stalled, it left behind a cast of political players, many of them neophytes to political administration. The country was well on its way to spiraling out of control.

It Helps to Have a Scorecard

In this political drama, a cast of characters took to the stage, including Patrice *Lumumba*, Prime Minister and African nationalist who was assassinated shortly after independence in 1961; General *Kasavubu*, who served as the first President of the Democratic Republic of the Congo until 1965; *Moise Tshombe*, a shrewd Congolese businessman and politician who served as President of the secessionist state of Katanga, then subsequently as Prime Minister; and lastly, perhaps the most well-known, General *Mobutu Sese Soko* and President of Zaire (formerly, the Democratic Republic of Congo) from 1965 to 1997.

In its most basic terms, the Congo state of crisis was a perpetual tripwire, a miniature Cold War played out between the United States, Russia, and their proxies. This proxy war, the so-called "conflict," eventually brought in the Belgians and their paratroopers, and, of course, the mercenaries from South Africa, always looking for a worthy fight at a princely sum. Cuba, aligned with Russia, was also on the ground. Ramon Benitez, aka Che Guevara, traveled to Congo in 1965 with twelve other Cubans and a small contingent of Afro-Cubans or Black Cubans as they were sometimes known. Che initially saw Lauren Kabila as someone who understood the fight against imperialism. It was a short-lived relationship, and the Che-Kabila honeymoon slowly faded. In the end, Che was disappointed with Kabila's undisciplined approach.

Not to be ignored is an important fact. The Congo was then, and still is today, extremely rich in strategic minerals such as cobalt, uranium, and industrial diamonds. Superpowers were salivating at the prospect of permanently controlling those resources.

The strategic minerals game had been in play since the 1940s when the United States attempted to stake a claim on uranium and cobalt mines to supply their effort in building an atomic bomb. The fate of the new country was at stake; that much was true, but the Western powers viewed the Congo as merely ground-zero in an ideological, cold war struggle with control over strategic resources best kept in the Western sphere. During this time, foreign intelligence agencies and their operatives in the Congo conducted many covert operations. The U.S. covert operations in the Congo focused on regime change, political action, air operations, and propaganda.

The Simba Rebellion

Between 1963 and 1965, there was a regional and bloody uprising called the Simba Rebellion. The name Simba, in Swahili, refers to an enormous lion. The Simba's, a quasi-Maoist revolutionary group, comprised mutineers, local tribesmen, and youth. They were fierce looking in one respect yet almost gruesomely comical in another. They wore brightly plumed headgear; some wore army fatigues, and others wore animal skins or loincloths. The only common element was that they were armed to the teeth with spears, machetes, old Belgian rifles, and whatever else they could find that could be used to kill. In some cases, Maoist indoctrination may have successfully energized the foot soldiers. Still, in most cases, they were drug-infused and strengthened in the belief that water, applied by a medicine man, would protect them from bullets.

By early 1964, mercenaries, led by "Mad Mike" Hoare and his primarily white army from central and southern Africa, had formed a unit known as *5 Commando ANC.* The team served as the spearhead of the ANC and was allegedly involved in unsanctioned killings, most likely in re-captured rebel areas.

By late 1964, the Simba's, in what may have been a last act of desperation in their short-lived terror campaign, had captured the city of Stanleyville, later known as Kisangani, after the Congolese National Army fled. The ANC's departure fundamentally left an open city with nearly 2000 unprotected Americans and Europeans who would soon be the Simba's bargaining chips.

I believe a book worth reading to help understand the events in Stanleyville is titled *111 Days in Stanleyville,* written by David Reed. I remember reading it many years ago and found it quite compelling, with a detailed account of the cold-blooded massacre in October of 1964 when 1,600 Europeans and Americans were held hostage by the Simba. A 1964 New York Times headline read, "28 More White Hostages Found Slain in Stanleyville; Toll in New Massacre May Reach 45." It was later determined that with the approaching Belgian paratroopers, the Simba slaughtered or wounded over 80 people in cold blood.

Knowing that the paratroopers were advancing, the Simba's gruesomely, brutally, and indiscriminately hacked their victims to death and shot others at point-blank range. Perhaps to better illustrate the savagery, here is a short piece taken from the newspaper Independent.co.uk where "Mad" Mike Hoare, the colorful mercenary, recounted the following shocking set of events: "The mayor of Stanleyville, *Sylvere Bondekwe,* a well-respected man, was forced to stand naked before a frenzied crowd of Simba rebels while one of them cut out his liver. The liver was given to the mob to eat, still hot and throbbing, as the victim died in agony before their eyes."

In another, the New York Times reported in November 1964 a gruesome incident where a woman "was weeping from grief, unable to, as she put it, "repress the vision" of rebel Jeunesse (Simba youth units) armed with spears and knives hacking to death her husband and her two sons."

"Mad Mike" Hoare, with his 300 or so mercenaries, played an integral part in *Operation Dragon Rouge* by rescuing many Congolese Roman Catholic nuns who, according to Chris Hoare, "were petrified with fear. Many wept copiously and had to be coaxed out of hiding."

My father told me at one time that he had met Mike Hoare, under what set of circumstances, how often, and exactly where, I do not know. My father held firm his "need to know" about his activities and to all others who inquired without a "need to know.) That is understandable, though in retrospect, with the passage of time, perhaps not.

I can only hazard a guess where the two might have met, including even a possible midnight visit at our home. Our phone had a habit of ringing one short rings, in the late evening. I could hear it from my bedroom: the sound of our front door being unbolted and opened, murmurs, then the study door closing. Repeat. Nevertheless, the Mike Hoare story is interesting, and like many of his contemporaries, the stories will remain unexplained, with minor footnotes to historical events long forgotten. Somewhere those answers are spelled out in typewritten reports and most surely tucked away with other files in a box in a government warehouse. Eventually, my generation will pass on, and there will no longer be that urgent need to find out what happened, when, and where. Historians in succeeding generations may find the answers that we could not.

In retrospect, the horrors of Stanleyville and post-Stanleyville were a far cry from the plush golf and waterskiing resort of the 1950s, where one mixed with the *beau-monde*. At that time, the well-known director, John Huston, had Katherine Hepburn and Humphrey Bogart on-site in Stanleyville to film part of *The African Queen*. For now, the bloodshed and horrors of 1964 Stanleyville had opened an ugly chapter whose wounds would not be so quickly closed.

As I recall, there were a fair number of students from our school whose parents were missionaries. Unsurprisingly, a missionary couple started the American School of Leopoldville. I can see our school superintendent's face as clearly today as I was there in the 1960s. Half or more of the student population had parents who lived deep in the bush, in lonely outposts doing God's work. This was a selfless calling of dedicated men and women working with the natives, preaching the Gospel, and helping to build churches and schools for the Congolese. I can think of no more dedicated people than these missionaries. I remember that some children lived with their parents in the "bush" and were likely home-schooled; I don't know. However, with the advent of the Simba rebellion in the mid-1960s, many missionaries hastily fled their missions deep in the bush well ahead of the Simba's bloody path. They returned to Leopoldville with their children with unimaginable tales of horror. I shall leave it at that.

One of the more unusual or bizarre occurrences during those crazy times (of which there seemed to have been plenty) occurred during one of our soccer games. Suddenly, our principal ran onto the field and waved everyone off the soccer field. Sure enough, within minutes, up in the sky, a large helicopter, a Chinook type, began maneuvering a careful descent and landing safely on the school field. The prop noise was deafening! The U.S. Government was testing if a helicopter of that size could land safely and swiftly begin an emergency rescue of all school children, though, most likely, our government's plan was only to evacuate American children leaving the remaining to fend for themselves. We had no firm idea how all of this would have played itself out other than to say we, as teenagers, were aware of the carnage in Stanleyville, having heard the horror stories told by many returning from the "bush."

Breaking Congo Curfew: Risky Business

One summer, the family, minus my father and older brother, enjoyed a month of family vacation (R&R) at my grandmother's seaside cottage in Cape May, New Jersey. It felt like I had escaped that steamy African country, swimming for miles, dodging man-eating alligators. You get the gist of it. I found a bit of Heaven right in New Jersey. I was back in America, with my cousins and had no intention of ever leaving. That thought ended abruptly. One day, as I was coming from the beach to have lunch, I met my aunt, who told me my father had been arrested! How does one respond to that news? I asked several questions and all I got was that my mother was on the phone with someone in Washington, DC.

To this day, I do not know the entire story, just bits, and pieces or as much as my father wanted to divulge. I starved for information. We learned that he was released shortly after his arrest. As I was led to understand, the sequence of events was that my father had a late evening appointment. Despite knowing full well there was a curfew, took a chance that he would not be stopped. Best laid plans of mice and men. He was arrested, seized, and ended up at a local military police barracks, familiar barracks to us as we drove past them daily on our way to school. Questions remain unanswered. Who knew about his whereabouts? Did our embassy play any part in effectuating his release? My father did not work for the embassy and enjoyed no special privileges. How did my father reach out to let anyone know he was there? Were there political connections at play and used? So I can only speculate on who, what, when, and where. I will never know the full details. I have a working theory that he made it known to the camp commander, that his good friend his good friend was President Mobutu's personal physician. Putting one's career against the President and his personal death squads might not be so appealing. Again, it's a theory and will stay as such. Years later, he added a few more tidbits of information and told me that as the soldiers lined him up along with various others who had been caught, he said, "I never felt as close to facing certain death as I did then."

While on this dark topic, I recall my brother saying that when he was visiting my father at his office, he recalls my father looking out the window to the parking lot below and saying something to the effect that "each time I cross the parking lot to go to my car I know I am a target."

"And at night the river would whisper to me, its voice a haunting echo of forgotten secrets." – *Heart of Darkness* by Joseph Conrad.

A Day in Downtown Kinshasa

"When I was a house staff, we didn't wake up with Vietnam and had
Cyprus for lunch and the Congo for dinner." Lyndon B. Johnson

It was business as usual with the ivory market up and running, selling all sorts of ivory gadgets. As shown in the photo
below, my parents once collected most of those same ivory pieces.
I remember all of them clearly. With time, some ivory pieces have
been spread amongst the children, others gifted or perhaps stolen.

I still have some pieces of art that are included in this book. Also, a few elegant ivory pieces or wooden statues, a malachite and ivory letter opener to open all my emails, and assorted trinkets such as a tribal knife, which never fails to intrigue my grandchildren. I have come up with more stories about that knife.

Today, while still functioning, the ivory market has gone underground to avoid government sanctions.

At the post office, crowds of children would gather around any car, hopefully, driven by a European, and try to sell single pieces of bubble gum held on a piece of cardboard like a silver tray. I can remember sitting in the car while my father went into the Post Office, usually on a business run of one sort or another. One amusing incident comes to mind. While we were in the car patiently waiting outside the post office, inside, a black hand reached out through the mailbox with three fingers rubbing together, the international sign for a "*mata bish*," a word in *Lingala* for "a tip." I would assume my father willingly put a few bills into the mysterious hand, a small price to pay in return for continued access to a special post office box. Outside, I would watch the Congolese children and recall that many had distended stomachs. This was most likely due to malnutrition, severe protein deficiency for starters, and a host of other ailments. You would sometimes see a hapless child suffering from dysentery, sitting on the sidewalk, barely moving. He would have colored-looking mucus slowly running from his nose and even an eye, and generally too weak to even brush away the hungry flies. Like so many children, he would undoubtedly have a short lifespan.

It was not unusual to see someone, usually an older man, with his hand or arm cut off at the elbow; the scene recalled the atrocities dispensed by the Congo's former Belgian colonial masters. One could only guess the cause of the mutilation. He most likely had worked on a rubber plantation somewhere deep in the bush. Maybe he had failed to meet his quota, and punishment was meted out. It was well known that under the Belgian regime, colonial masters would cut off the hands of their workers, dead or alive. This proved to their Belgian colonial administrators that punishment had been meted out but their bullets, in short supply, had not gone to waste. Make every bullet count.

The scenes I have described in downtown Leopoldville were hardly an exception but rather typical of some of the daily sights, which I shall spare you further details.

In the center of Kinshasa was an excellent restaurant called "*Au Plein Vent*," a somewhat whimsical name, as there was hardly a breeze to be found but certainly in spirit. The restaurant was on the seventh floor of an apartment building, providing diners with a panoramic view of Kinshasa by night, with lights twinkling everywhere. Just beyond the Congo River, towards the other side, one could just make out the lights of Brazzaville. The restaurant had a wonderful and colorful menu ranging from the house specialty, *fondue Savoyard,* to local spicy chicken dishes. Of course, everything was served in true Belgian tradition, including pile-high platters of French fries or *frites.* Dinner was washed down with a cold local beer or a Danish import at three times the price. The restaurant, I understand from talking to an old Congo hand, has finally closed its doors.

The Chicken and the Python

View of our old school in Leo II before the new one was built in *Ngaliema*.

$\mathcal{T}$his story is genuinely African in every sense.

As usual, our driver, Prosper, dropped us off at school. He was truly likable fellow and certainly more trustworthy than his predecessors who used our car as a taxi. For some reason, my father reached under the seat only to find a cardboard sign with

Taxi crudely written on it. That ended the short-lived career of that driver. Enterprising, I will give him that much.

After Prosper left us, we climbed up the steps to the school. We noticed that a crowd of students had gathered near a palm tree. You could sense the excitement in the air. Something was up, and we were not about to miss out on whatever that was. As I pushed past my classmates, I remembered seeing a giant snake, thick and round. In the middle of the snake was a considerably large bump which I was told was an undigested chicken swallowed whole before the chicken could cross the road to safety. The snake was a Central African rock python. It is regarded as one of the larger snake species in the world, approaching up to twenty feet in length.

Despite not attacking humans, an interesting report in the 1979 Journal of Herpetology about a Central African rock python killing a 13-year-old South African who died from suffocation and internal injuries. Now this. After killing the python, they noticed the victim's head was covered in saliva. Yes, you all know where this is going. It was thought that had the python not been interrupted, the snake would have succeeded in swallowing the 90-pound boy. From head to toe.

After a while, we left as it was class time. We knew the locals would undoubtedly cut it up and probably have the chicken for dinner. By recess, all evidence of the snake and the chicken was gone. Little more was left other than a good story.

A Christmas Morning

Merry Christmas!

*Y*e 'Olde Christmas carolers, the ones we fondly remember spreading Christmas Eve cheer door to door were in short supply. However, stockings were hung with care around the living room. Even though we had only some elements of the holidays, we were guaranteed a special Christmas morning celebration. They announced their presence on the front patio with their drums.

We obliged and went outside, some of us in our best breakfast attire, all waiting for the inevitable show. Some had spears, others decorated shields, colorful armbands, and elaborate headgear. All had faces painted. Colorful? Yes, to be sure, and one kept a safe distance while those spears were bandied about. After much guttural noise, hands and feet gesticulating, dancing, jumping about, and beating on their shields with their spears, the dancers and all the guttural sounds finally stopped. We all clapped that it was finally over. My father, who seemed to enjoy the dancers perhaps more than the rest of us, pulled out his wallet and gave the leader a generous tip to share with his fellow dancers. A tip that was more than enough to pay for several rounds of beers, if not more.

It was Christmas, after all.

LIVING THE LIFE, CONGO-STYLE

I am confident that expats, around the world, be they in Cairo, Istanbul, Saigon, or Kinshasa will always get together for quiet dinners with friends or cocktail parties. My parents put on some of the most elegant and successful cocktail parties I have ever witnessed. So, I tip my hat to them wherever they may be, undoubtedly looking down at me and shaking their heads, acknowledging that this child was always a bit different from the others. I remember well those last few moments before the first guests arrived. It was as if a movie director had just shouted, "Everyone, please take your places and action!" At that moment, the guests were ushered in and greeted warmly. Yours truly, at one time or another, would have been shanghaied as a coat runner up several flights of stairs (as in Antwerp) or running with drink orders to the bar on the porch in our home in Kinshasa; I would eventually be mixing cocktails for the guests. I recall that the ladies were always decked out "to the nines," as they say, and looked like a million dollars. I would go from guest to guest, "May I refill your glass?" The not-unusual answer, in a gravely cigarette and Scotch-laced voice was, "Oh, you're so sweet, I would love another Scotch!"

As I mentioned earlier, our house had a veranda that ran the back length of the house, the bar was set up at one end, and my two older brothers and I, all at one time, acted as bartenders. Almost sixty years ago, I can vividly recall the scene: Cha-cha music from the old record player and alcohol flowing endlessly. All under a cloud of blue cigarette smoke, heady perfume, business attire, diplomats, businessmen, occasional members of the missionary community, French and English language used freely, Americans and Europeans all with a sense of devil-may-care what tomorrow brings; and yes, I will have another Scotch. Make sure you have your passport ready and know the location of your assembly point. Everyone knew that hell might break loose. But for now, party on!

Rear view of our house on Chemin des Dames

Neighbors

Our little neighborhood on *Chemin des Dames* was simple and unassuming. I remember there was one American family down the road; the father was attached to the U.S. Army as I recall. We boys all had, at one time or another, been babysitters. I remember our immediate neighbors quite clearly. They were a Dutch family of three. As I recall, they had lived in the then-Dutch East Indies, presumably in Jakarta. With the outbreak of the second world war, the family got swept up by the Japanese Army and interned in a camp for the duration of the war. The husband was a gregarious fellow; I can picture him today; with a hearty deep laugh, and he always appreciated a cold Heineken. We rarely saw his daughter, who occasionally ventured outside but only with her mother. I recall seeing her just a few times —a lovely young lady who must have been in her late twenties or early thirties. I can only surmise that life interned under the Japanese thumb, had been stressful beyond words and, at times, even brutal. Over time, I am sure it took its toll. For her, I imagine, staying inside must have been a safer alternative to venturing outside. I think I can understand that.

For the life of me, I cannot recall our other neighbors, but I do remember there was a house further down the street where, for some insane reason, my older was on the roof and, as things happen, he fell through the roof and landed in a bedroom, right between two beds.

On occasion, my friend who had access to a Ford Cortina would get behind the wheel along with four others. We drove into downtown Leopoldville to a joint called *Le Scotch Club*. Open twenty-fours with music, drinks, and bar girls. For a fifteen or sixteen-year-old, what's not to like? We drank beers and danced with the bar girls.

Near the end of our tour in Kinshasa, my greatest desire was to leave yesterday. I can't point to one or several incidents; instead, it was an accumulated feeling of desperation. Was it perhaps the general political unrest not knowing what tomorrow might bring, was it the helicopter practice landing on our soccer field should the student body (or most likely, just the Americans) need to be quickly evacuated, or was this malaise from the extreme abject poverty and disease that we witnessed day after day? I don't know; it could have been triggered when I was listening to the radio and heard someone screaming, *"il faut tuer tout les blancs"* or "We must kill all the whites." I was not a political analyst, not even an aspiring one, so I could not put any of what I heard into some meaningful context, but I do know that it only served to add to my growing sense of uneasiness and, yes, perhaps even a sense of desperation.

Departure Time

Before our departure, my parents invited the staff and their wives for a farewell tea/drink. My mind goes blank on the details of that event. I can almost picture my parents playing host to their invitees, likely feeling as uncomfortable as they were. It was an amicable parting gesture.

I clearly remember the day we were set to return to the United States. I was sure something would happen that would delay our departure. I felt as if there was this cloud hovering over me that would intervene at the last minute. As I write this, I can't remember if we said goodbye to the staff: Albert and Emanuel, our faithful houseboys; Gaston, the gardener; Vincent, our night watchman and Prosper, our driver. I can imagine they must have been saddened to see us go. For the most part, we had all been together for five years, give or take a couple of drivers, and we shared the good and the difficult times. A few days before we left, I recall one of my father's colleagues came by in a pickup truck and took away several pieces of furniture. As he left, I remember him, his hand waving in the air as he roared down our street, "*Chemin.*" Years later, I remember reading about that same person and learned that he eventually rose to a very senior position with the same government agency he had so honorably served for many years. He passed away just a few years ago.

We left the house and drove down our street, *Chemin des Dames,* for the last time. I did not turn around for a final look. Any sentimental feelings had long since disappeared. I wanted out. The Congo, however, does not easily relinquish its grip on those who wish to leave. On our way to the airport, we got a flat tire. Someone, I don't recall who, suggested it was most likely the chauffeur who had sabotaged the tire. This was not out of malice but because he was so devoted to us and did not want us to leave.

As we passed through customs at *N'djili* Airport, I held my breath as my anxiety rose, sensing inevitable doom. Something would indeed happen, and at any moment, we could be pulled aside, and my father interrogated for some lame reason. We would eventually miss our flight. Congo wins again! Would it be the ivory cane my father carried with him, or something else? It was not until our plane had taken off and we were finally airborne that I began to feel a growing sense of deep, welcomed relief.

A Congo Postscript

Modern-day Kinshasa

With time and maturity, my years in Congo were remembered as challenging. But those years were also eye-opening and humbling. The people I encountered, the friends I made, many of whom I am still thankfully in touch with on social media. All were of sterling character. Many have returned to the Congo, many never left but all are doing worthwhile things. I think about our houseboys, who were so welcoming and kind from the first morning I saw them until the day we left. Now, I want to learn about their culture, struggles, and resilience in a way that I could never have imagined possible.

I was anxious to leave the Congo; in some strange way, I knew it was time to embrace another chapter, another adventure, one that would start first with our return to the United States and our return to Belgium, a year later. On our return flight from the Congo in 1968, we learned about Bobby Kennedy's assassination. I still recall where we were in Leopoldville that day in 1963. We were watching an outdoor movie at the Canadian Embassy. The film stopped, and it was announced that John F. Kennedy had been assassinated. We seemed destined to live in a time of despair with only just a little hope.

In retrospect, I was grateful for the opportunity to experience something so very unique. The Congo has its exceptional beauty, and I was thankful to have experienced at least some of it. In my later worldwide travels, I would see or experience many things that often reminded me of my days in the Congo. It never leaves you, even if you would want it to.

One day, I promise myself, I shall return. I must.

THE MAN IN THE SEERSUCKER SUIT

A Short Story

"If Congo deteriorates and Western influence fades rapidly, the Bloc will have a feast and not need to work very hard for it." Chief of CIA's Africa Division, 1960.

The cabin lights came on along with a matter-of-fact voice:

"Good evening, ladies, and gentlemen. This is First Officer Miller speaking from the cockpit. We are beginning our descent to Uhuru National Airport, where the temperature is 89 degrees, and humidity is a welcoming 98 degrees with light rain. We have an estimated arrival time of 10:30 PM and look forward to getting you folks on the ground as quickly as possible. We wish you a pleasant journey on behalf of Pan American Airways and your cabin crew. Please ensure your table trays are stored securely upright in a locked position; a stewardess will come by one last time with customs forms. Once again, it's been our pleasure flying with you." "Bonsoir Mesdames, messieurs, nous allons atterrir dans quelques minutes à l'aéroport international…"

inston Harrison George III – better known to his friends and prep school chums simply as "Winnie" – felt ready for his first overseas post. As far as the company was concerned, specifically those on the Africa desk, he was fit for duty, which was good enough. All his fitness reports and performance evaluations spoke highly of him, and he had the requisite skills to operate in the field. His orders were cut, he followed the checklist and met with Personnel on family issues, leave accumulation, direct deposit instructions, retirement accounts, and travel plans, and updated his last will, detail after detail after detail, and that didn't even include the intricate operational procedures that went with his new status as AgroLan International's Vice President for Marketing and Business Development. Agro was a Midwest grain exporting company head-quartered in Lincoln, Nebraska, with another main office in New York City. It handled a busy international export business in several countries in the developing world and was closely connected with the now ballooning AID program earmarked for Africa. Philip Johns, President, and CEO, a World War II veteran and graduate of the elite School of Diplomacy in Washington, DC, built the company from the ground up. He traveled regularly between his Upper East Side home in New York City and the sprawling corporate campus in Lincoln. Winnie met Philip once in New York City over dinner. He was pleased to learn they attended the same prep school in New Hampshire and were on the varsity crew team. He liked Philip immediately and felt a bond had been forged.

Over the last few months, Winnie had watched enough grainy footage of violent urban crowds unleashed in the streets; groups of young men throwing rocks and systematically ransacking businesses, firing guns in the air; footage of frightened and con-fused-looking whites, Europeans, huddled together, some hold-ing bloody handkerchiefs to their heads; local mobs chanting "death-death-death to colonialism" and "long live the revolu-tion" or carrying banners with Marxist party slogans promising a brighter future for all *citoyens*. The scene was repeated almost daily along the newly renamed Boulevard du Premier Mai, the main thoroughfare in the city. Grainy footage shot at the *Aeroport Occidentale,* now renamed Uhuru National Airport, in a fit of rev-olutionary fervor, showed a gauntlet of locals taunting, touching, and pushing. They were trying to reach out and grab suitcases and bags belonging to anxious passengers as they arrived. Winnie had read countless telex messages, cables, and reports via Diplomatic Pouch from the station and the Embassy, which read in some places like a horror story describing matter of fact, cars travel-ing on the airport road being indiscriminately stopped and pulled over with one or two occupants dragged out and beaten senseless. He had read reams of intelligence reports, political assessments on Sino-Soviet dominance and influence, political and psychological profiles of the current leadership, economic analyses from various Washington think tanks and universities, and even Congressional testimony from a panel of carefully selected experts, along with just about any other piece of information he could lay his hands on, was digested with a sense of urgency.

There was one clear fact: Winnie was more than itching to leave Room 253-E. He was sick and tired and restless for an as-signment. His windowless office, his cell, was closing in on him by the minute. His office, located along the East wing of the com-plex, was about as far removed from anything and about a mile away from the cafeteria. This had been his office for almost six months, and as homes went, it was about the best a GS-9 could expect or hope for.

Sparsely furnished with a somber-looking grey metal desk and chair placed squarely in the middle of the room, one authorized metal grey visitor's chair, and one round metal grey wastebasket. Departmental policies and procedures allowed him a grey metal bookcase with two adjustable shelves which held an internal departmental phone book with specific directions on dialing between bureaus and offices, a government phone book, the ever-present GPO manual, a style guide to effective writing (condition like new) and a beat-up DC – Maryland- Virginia phone book thoughtfully left by some previous tenant also looking to escape. His phone was a black rotary, with a white sticker in the middle of the dial with 253-E faintly typed on. When the phone rang, he answered "253-E" just as he was supposed to. By the door was also a metal coat hanger with a wooden hanger, *Snow White Dry Cleaners Alexandria, Virginia*, stamped on it. Overhead the fluorescent light was missing two of the three lights, but he had been assured his office was scheduled for a maintenance visit almost any day now. One standard gooseneck desk lamp gave him the only source of light to read, re-read and study. Some enterprising civil servants before him had dared to take the initiative and hung a cork bulletin board. This was now well-worn in several places but still held a few complimentary thumbtacks. A small personal desk calendar was on his desk, sandwiched between the" In-Out" trays. It had a picture of his wife looking shyly away, taken last summer, and one of the two children in their new Christmas outfits sitting and smiling for the Montgomery Wards photographer and a caption at the bottom, in gold lettering: *Christmas 1961.*

Winnie attended an exclusive boy's school on the Upper East in New York City until he was ready to prep. His parents then dutifully placed him at a New Hampshire-exclusive preparatory school, a feeder school for the Ivy Leagues. The very same school his grandfather and Father had proudly attended. By all accounts and judging by the headmaster's comments, Winnie did well, earning high marks in most, if not all, of his studies. He was team captain of the school's crew team, where he was the stroke on a four-man shell. He was also a member of the French Drama Club and the Chess Club. In 1957 Winnie received his Bachelor of Arts degree with High Honors from Princeton University's Woodrow Wilson School of Public and International Affairs. Winnie was in England three months later on a Rhodes Scholarship to Oxford. He had been told that Saigon station was the most logical overseas career move given his strength with the French language as well as his Asian studies while at Oxford. However, everything had changed; now the Africa Desk in Washington, DC, and Congo station were ramping up as fast as they could to "get up to speed," and duty station papers were being re-routed from one part of the world to a new flash point in the heart of Africa.

The Pan American Airways Jet Clipper flight 156 from New York La Guardia touched down at Uhuru National Airport. Looking out his window, as the plane approached the terminal, Winnie noticed two Soviet Antonov An-12s and a Shaanxi Y-8, a Chinese version of an Antonov, on the other side of the runway, refueling. A crew stood nearby. No one seemed to be in a hurry. When Winnie, in his grey seersucker suit, tie shoes, white shirt, and black knit tie and holding his hat and briefcase, stepped out into the African heat, it was as if he had entered a sauna. The heat was more than oppressive, it was oven-like, and the humidity grabbed him by the throat, clamped his chest, and descended on him like a cloak, sapping what energy he had left from his eighteen-hour flight. He had arrived. Already, "back home" seemed like thousands of miles and another world away.

Once inside the poorly ventilated terminal, Winnie passed through customs. He showed his passport and World Health shot records and answered the perfunctory questions as to the purpose of his visit. He was looked at for a moment, then compared to his photo, the official's yellowed eyes carefully looking at him; he sighed then stamped Winnie's passport and gave him a big smile as if to say, "I could have made things very uncomfortable for you, but you lucked out." The crowd in the terminal was a mixture of Anglos, Indians, Orientals, Middle Eastern types, Portuguese, and several African nationals from various other countries. All mixed in the African heat. All are amassing in front of a slowing conveyor belt, dragging their suitcases or cardboard wrapped tightly with rope. It had the making of a hideous carnival or a terrible movie. Patrolling lazily among the passengers were paramilitary police teams of young men with oversized, over-starched uniforms, their helmets practically covering their eyes, an automatic machine gun loosely held and ready. They would not hesitate to use extreme force if necessary, not always for a good reason.

Winnie, jacket over one arm, shirt dripping wet, sleeves rolled up to the elbow, and tie loosened at the neck, searched the crowd for a familiar face or the contact who knew him. At last, he saw a large balding man wearing a short-sleeve plaid button-down shirt, jeans, and cowboy boots whom he recognized as having attended briefings in Washington. Sam carried a sign: "Passenger George, AgroLan Company." Sam saw him and smiled, "Welcome to your new home away from home; I dare say, Winnie, you may have just turned the corner into hell!" They both made their way out of the terminal, pushing through a crowd of stick-like children with bloated stomachs, threadbare shorts, and shoe-less, all with their hands out, begging for a little something, anything. Sam threw the bags in the back of his old UN Land Rover Jeep and drove away from the airport, surprising the guards who were busy talking to a few local girls hanging around the entrance hoping to catch a lonely customer. Once on the airport road, Sam reached into his boot and pulled out a pistol. He placed it between them, reached under his seat, and brought out two bottles of lukewarm local beer. Cheers Mate!

SOUTH AFRICA

Cape Town, the Mother City

View of Table Mountain in the far distance

On a business trip some years ago, which took me, among others, to South Africa, I found myself in Cape Town. This is the jewel of a town with some of the most delightful people you could imagine meeting. I would remind you that not far from Cape Town in the wine valley is the beautiful *Franschhoek*

(French Corner) Valley in which French Huguenot refugees initially settled. Of course, it is the home of some of the finest wines I've ever tasted outside of France. But that wine-tasting adventure is a story for another time. For now, back to some speedy food and the Cape.

OSTRICH PIE IS BEST SERVED AT 3500 FEET ABOVE SEA LEVEL

he key to a successful ostrich pie is catching the bird. I do not say that lightly either. Most well-meaning people ask how difficult can it be to catch a flightless bird. I point out that if they can run faster than the bird, which would be approximately 40 miles per hour, than they are in luck! While in Cape Town, I first tasted ostrich pie at a little restaurant on Table Mountain, 3500 feet above sea level. A less-than-reassuring cable ride up the mountain is certainly not for the faint of the heart. I thought the revolving floor added such a nice touch as my stomach turned and twisted in so many strange, unimaginable ways. Once you reach your destination, with wobbly legs and all, the view overlooking Cape Town, Cable Bay, and the Cape Peninsula is breathtaking in every sense. You can't stop taking photos; it was heaven for a photo junkie like me. Sitting on the ledge might have given me a better shot, but I wanted to live a little longer and left my parachute back at the hotel.

I was pleased to find a quaint little eatery called the Table Mountain Café (how did they come up with that name?) with a beautiful view, but their floor did not turn, which I thought was a nice touch. The food is unpretentious and excellent, the staff is super friendly, and the wine is very local. I spun a quick yarn for the wait staff, telling them that years ago, I was a young boy, my brothers and I used to race each other on ostriches, hanging on for dear life as the beast dashed across the field, unfortunately never in the right direction. I hoped they had not seen an old classic, The Swiss Family Robinson. I'm sure my story made quite an impression and likely not one I would have found particularly endearing.

LUNCH IN THE FRANSCHHOEK WINE VALLEY

$\mathcal{A}$ small piece of heaven is situated approximately one hour from Cape Town. I hesitate to say more because why ruin it with an onslaught of tourists looking for a tasty hamburger, a plateful of fries, and a cheap wine? Non et non! This little piece of heaven is called *La Petite Ferme*, or the "small farm" perched on the Franschhoek Mountains in the Western Cape wine valley. The farm is ready and eagerly awaits the discerning customer or overnight guest. I am not sure what impressed me the most. Perhaps it was the view, arguably jaw-dropping, or maybe the menu and the incredible South African wine? You can understand my predicament.

I was there for lunch and I would have stayed until dinner but that was not possible. It killed me. For lunch, I had Karoo Lamb (branded as House classic), rolled lamb shoulder rolled in phyllo, and roasted *aubergine* puree. While loosening my belt and readying myself for dessert, I observed what looked like a baboon lumbering near the restaurant. Then, to my surprise, it climbed up and sat on one of the gate posts. I thought I was hallucinating, so I inquired with our waiter, who told me that there were baboons who strolled the vineyard and seemed to preferred a good Pinot Noir grape but enjoyed the Chardonnay grapes. I mulled that over but could not fault the baboon's choice of grapes.

For dessert, I recall succumbing to the Cape brandy pudding. I confess, just the name alone called out to me. It could have been a bow of Jell-O, but no, it was a dessert of the Gods: Hazelnut ice cream, spiced berry compote, and vanilla crème anglaise. It was one of those desserts that, you tell yourself, I could quite easily suffer through another one. I think we've all been there at one time or another.

It was time for a cappuccino with a view and, perhaps, a short siesta. But where was that baboon?

If you are contemplating a visit to South Africa, make sure you carve out some time to visit and enjoy Cape Town and the wine valley, including Franschhoek.

INDIA

By the 19th century, Great Britain had become the dominant political power on the subcontinent, and India was seen as the "Jewel in the Crown" of the British Empire. Years of nonviolent resistance to British rule eventually resulted in Indian independence in 1947. (CIA Factbook)

Delhi In Four Parts

Delhi is my emotional home; I still dream of owning a house there.
—Kabir Bedi

Episode 1: Arriving in Delhi, More Dead Than Alive

$\mathcal{S}$omehow, I made it to Delhi in one piece after many hours in a plane. I felt like a towel that was wrung out to dry but never does. My arrival at Delhi's Indira Gandhi International Airport was viewed through a comatose lens. I had not slept for a long time, but more likely, just a couple of sleepless travel days. Initially, the airport seemed eerily quiet, as if no one had told us that Delhi was closed for the season. I spoke too soon, for I was about to witness an army of human ants crawling everywhere, over everything and into anything. It was a rude slap in the face and a lesson well learned for this global traveler. I scanned the sea of faces in the arrival lounge, hoping to see my name scrawled on a placard or something similar. This process had become an all too familiar drill. Finally, after walking the rope to and from and scanning the various signs, a welcoming face in a hotel uniform appeared, holding a vinyl card with the hotel and my name on it.

My driver. "Naresh," introduced me to his superior, a serious, no-nonsense fellow whose job, I presume, was to ensure the orderly pick-up of passengers at the airport was accomplished. He shook my hand; it was more like me shaking a limp, gloved, unresponsive appendage. He wished me a pleasant stay, then disappeared in the rowd to find the next arrival. I watched as he plunged into the mass of Indians, anxious passengers, and everyone else, all pushing and shoving for no apparent reason—just the Indian way.

As my driver and I emerged from the airport terminal into the sunlight, it was as if a two-by-four hit me over the head. It was like putting your head in an oven, then adding around 90% humidity, and you almost have it. It took me back to my years in Africa, in the heart of darkness! It was monsoon season here, the humidity was ever present, and you were constantly reminded each time you breathed in Delhi air. Street vendors were hawking iced "bottled water" and juice drinks of undetermined varieties and origins. Others had mystery meat on skewers. What animal got run over, I wondered?

Everything around me was slowly becoming a gradual rote. People seemed to mill aimlessly about. Drivers of cars, Tuk-Tuks, motorcycles, trucks and buses big and small, leaned on their horns, hoping against hope to urge traffic forward. Doing so gave them a sense that they could control something in their lives, no matter how small or inconsequential. Traffic was not going to move forward with any speed, anytime soon. The cacophony sound of horns, frantic bicycle bells, and car engines gunning, combined with the overwhelming smell of gasoline and diesel truck fumes mixed with the smell of charcoal, the pungent, rancid smell of the masses shoved together, the smell of overripen fruit long gone bad but still being sold, left you stupefied, in a cultural shock, your senses brutally assaulted like never before. I don't wish to seem too colonial, but this scene had all the familiar trappings of a third-world country. Seeing this, it was a little hard to believe that India had put a rocket into space and perhaps soon would land one on the moon, and with my total admiration and congratulations. The other shoe was about to drop, one that was less exciting and staring me in the face.

Masses of humanity sizzling in the tropics with more than a fair share of military police armed with machine guns at the ready; they looked bored and seemed to be just wandering aimlessly about, perhaps waiting for a fender bender or a smuggler on the run, anything to distract them from the ceaseless, never-ending boredom of everyday life.

Naresh screeched the black Toyota to a halt, jumped out, and immediately offered me an iced cold bottle of water that looked to be authentic (Note: please check back with me in 36 hrs. to see if anything has incubated). He then jumped behind the wheel (on the right-hand side) and, quite ceremoniously, pulled on a pair of white gloves and donned his plebe-like white hat. I thought he would ask me to dance. I was slowly turning into a prune. Finally, the AC groaned, then slowly kicked in with a full blast of fabricated cold air.

I began to get a general idea about traffic and drivers ignoring traffic lanes (lanes for what?) and red lights (again, for what?) as we slowly left the airport, five lanes converging into two until we reached a toll booth manned by some serious looking officials picking their teeth and checking to see if there was any action in the cars passing by; again, waiting for something to happen. Anything.

On learning that I was even remotely interested in Delhi, Naresh saw an opportunity to make a few extra rupees. He gave me a nickel tour. Nothing wrong with the Indian entrepreneurial spirit. He started pointing out landmarks right and left and turned his attention back to traffic only when necessary. Sitting in the front seat, I watched my life pass before my eyes repeatedly. I don't know how best to describe the lunacy; as I said earlier, you have motorcycles, sometimes with three or four passengers, bicycles with two adult passengers and a naked little child straddling the bike with daddy, trucks that were filled beyond imagination, and then, my favorite invention which the Indians call the "tuk-tuk." These modern-day rickshaws with plastic roofs, open side doors, a small engine that might have worked well on a lawn mower, and enough room in the back for one Westerner or five Indians comfortably.

Tuk-tuks, those motorized baby carriages, were everywhere; some looked like they'd been held together with baling wire. They played chicken with buses, cars, and motorbikes with reckless abandonment in the Delhi traffic mixing bowl. Everyone was honking their horns and playing the same Indian-chicken game. Nothing made sense in this roller derby from Hell other than the sure knowledge that standing still would be suicide. With everyone leaning on their horns, humanity's mechanized mass slowly progressed.

EPISODE 2: DELHI
REVEALS HERSELF

I finally arrived at my hotel after enduring a little more sightseeing. In my near sleepless trance, I was nevertheless able to appreciate and admire the broad boulevards and the architecture in this district of New Delhi known as the "diplomatic enclave," which includes a litany of consulates and embassies, elegant hotels, government buildings, international schools, senior-ranking military housing, and officers' clubs. All of these were located near well-known landmarks such as India Gate, the President's tiny home with 24 bedrooms and not to be ignored, easy distance to Khan Market, a necessary stop for me to buy Christmas presents.

After a quick look into the trunk and under the hood, the hotel security team rolled the furniture out of our way. We were now inside the compound. As you can see, security was rigorously tight!

I was greeted at the front steps by a colorful display of employees. Some wore the richly colored, traditional Indian garb, but all with hands together in an expression of welcome and blessing beyond *Namaste*. The hotel staff soon had me seated in a comfortable chair at a large table and quickly presented with a glass of jasmine tea and a cookie. At the same time, my passport was reviewed for authenticity and other hotel formalities. You felt as if they were over-functioning. The option to impeccable service is being relegated to picking up invisible pieces of something, anything from the hotel's immaculate front lawn. There are always staff working the lawns, carefully looking for anything suspicious or perhaps a blade of grass out of place. Despite being deprived of sleep, I had a pleasant dinner in a lovely outdoor setting. This was done with service at your beck and call and fabulous food to match!

India Gate

Monday morning started off with a bang. Early breakfast meeting with two business contacts: One representing my home state's India office, the other from the U.S. Embassy's U.S. Commercial Service in Delhi. Following a detailed briefing and

213

Q&A, I was on the road to my first appointment, located in South Delhi. In other words, I had to cross Hell to get there during an insane but otherwise quite normal Delhi rush hour. The same cast of characters was present: Bicycles, the motorbikes, scooters, the little "tuk-tuks," the dilapidated trucks, cars, and hopelessly overloaded buses, all twisting and turning from one traffic lane to the next, irrespective of traffic lights, roads, signals, pedestrians or even an occasional poor traffic cop trying his best to stem the tide of humanity. I mentioned somewhat sarcastically, "Thank goodness for the traffic cop." My driver answered: "Yes, thank goodness he's there because if someone broke down, it would be a traffic nightmare." I nodded and kept quiet and pondered the absurdity of that remark. For a moment, I pondered what Kafka might have said about this tangled mass of man and machine. A woman looking quite miserable and desperate, holding in her arms a malnourished infant, ribcage all too visible and looking resigned, approached the taxicab, scratched a fingernail on the windowpane, clearly begging for anything. I may have finally found my very own Heart of Darkness.

On occasion, you see a water buffalo cross the street. I don't know what else to say about that other than to note that it's certainly different. I had no idea the buffalo could distinguish between red and green lights. It's like the monkeys crossing the street two by two. I recalled seeing one wearing a backpack.

EPISODE 3: MONKEYS STORM PARLIAMENT NEWS AT ELEVEN

I previously mentioned the infamous monkeys strolling about Delhi, two by two, as if the city belonged to them. I understood from my guide that because they were increasingly seen as a public nuisance, the Delhi government, in a carefully planned, top-secret counterterrorism plan, hired a special operations team of monkeys – the Langur – a much larger "badass" monkey. Their mission was to drive the Rhesus monkeys out of Parliament, then out of ministry buildings, and finally pushed well past the comfortable, leafy living quarters of senior government officials, those most offended by the monkey takeover.

Despite concerted efforts by the Langur monkeys, the pesky Rhesus returned each night, encouraged by offerings of food such as bananas and peanuts from their local supporters. The food supply was left by Hindus, who viewed monkeys as living incarnations of the monkey god Hanuman. In the past, according to the Hindu Times, packs of monkeys had broken into the Parliament (shall we call this a riot, then?) and invaded the prime minister's office and defense ministry, ripping up wiring and tearing through files, perhaps looking to see what information the government had collected on them. Humans who dared to resist were sometimes bitten – or worse. They treated the Indian Parliament building as a playground, much like our legislators do in Washington. In the process, they showed little respect for public law and order. In a bold, strategic move, the monkeys at one point even invaded the prime minister's office and the Defense Ministry. Then, to add insult to injury, the now infamous monkeys would stroll about Delhi, two by two, as if the city belonged to them. The fruits of victory are sweet.

I've asked people in Delhi about the monkey uprising, and they would nod in the affirmative. "Oh well, you know, the monkey plays a significant role in Hindi mythology." I gather the monkeys are not planning on leaving the halls of power in Delhi anytime soon.

In another edition of Ripley's Believe it or Not, last night, I was on my balcony around early AM, surveying the tranquil street below, now peacefully quiet from the incessant honking of car horns. What did my wandering eyes behold? A pack of 4 substantial spotted grey dogs, let's say a bit smaller than a greyhound, casually strolling up the sidewalk, then deciding it was time to cross the street, one, then two, then the rest following leisurely behind. The pack leader decided now was the perfect time and place to "take five" in the middle of the intersection. Then came the inevitable sound of car horns and tires screeching as drivers swerved around the pack. The dogs were not the least phased, brazen as they were, much like the rhesus monkeys. Maybe this was big dog territory, I don't know; I had not been briefed. I recounted this story to an Indian, and he had a good laugh. "Ah yes, well, you know, dogs are very important to the Indians." I love dogs too, but I could not see a pack of dogs roaming about freely in downtown Annapolis or, God forbid, Washington, DC, and stopping traffic (there is the actual crime!) But then, I could not see a pack of monkeys on the loose, either.

It rained last night, not a gentle sprinkle, but it was as if God had opened the world's fire hydrants and directed them toward Delhi. When everything stopped, I stepped out onto the porch—another of my sleepless nights. Yes, the streets were clean, and the dust disappeared, but just as quickly, the humidity rapidly rose to an atrocious level. It took your breath away and locked you in place. As they say, it was so thick you could cut it with a knife. Ice, please?

I had a business meeting in another part of Delhi. In addition to the expected tangled morning rush hour mess, the rains from the previous night had hammered the roads, some saying a fond farewell as they slipped away. It made for a fascinating ride, with the mechanized wave groaning slowly forward to the incessant sound of honking motorbikes, cars, trucks, and bicycles. The occasional rapping of a beggar's fingernail on my window would break up the scenery. A toothless plea for a crumb of anything. "Can't you see I'm trying to take your picture? No sense of decency at all!" After a while, I recall telling my colleague that the shock of seeing someone thin as a reed and holding a child even lighter eventually wears off. You become numb just as I ultimately became numb witnessing the incredible poverty in a country like the Congo.

On one occasion, my well-meaning American colleague cracked open a window and slipped a U.S. one-dollar bill. The cab driver almost had a fit and ordered the window shut. If not, he told us, every single beggar and wretch, old and young in Delhi, would descend on his cab. A lesson well learned for someone who is not used to the peculiarities of developing countries. An incident that I knew was bound to happen.

Old Delhi has a certain charm. I had forgotten that one could miss Delhi (and in this case, North Delhi – a treat!), even though it had only been three months ago. The incredible heat, the smog, dust, unparallel traffic congestion, a mass of humanity, cars, buses, tuck-tucks pushing and shoving for space, the apparent signs of incredible poverty, and a few more lovely attributes which escape me. When your cab driver repeatedly asks if you want to turn around now and return to the hotel, he probably wonders what this silly foreigner thinks he's doing.

Leaving the cool confines of my hotel in Delhi's Diplomatic Enclave, I stepped out onto the hotel's neatly manicured gardens that are constantly attended to. The temperature was chilly 113 degrees but bearable for some insane reason. After a few cold Gin and Tonics, things started to look up, and you could think about the evening ahead.

Soon, a nicely chilled bottle of Sauvignon Blanc would be brought to my tent, and I would be asked if dinner reservations were required. Of course, my answer was in the affirmative. I should have added, "Do make sure the horses are watered and taken care of; we travel to Rajasthan tomorrow in open country; anything can happen." I realized I had left my pith helmet in my room; I would not need it for dinner.

EPISODE 4: SO LONG TO DELHI

On my last day in Delhi, since I had no business appointments, I naturally scheduled a short tour with my trusty driver, aka tour guide, and his working English, which was far superior to my Hindi. The humidity was a killer, and even the locals agreed.

My first stop of interest was the renowned "Red Fort" – red because it was built with red sandstone hundreds of years ago by the ruling families and eventually taken over by the British in 1947. Later it became an Indian garrison and was eventually deeded to the state. It is an impressive structure, to be sure, and defies comprehension.

It was a military fort built a hundred years ago and still has that feel. As the cavalry rode past me, their horse's hooves making a racket on the pavement, for a moment, I was transported back in time somewhere lost in an adventure story about India. I thought I recognized young Winston as a Lancer, but I was mistaken. These days, the fort is heavily armed in anticipation of national celebrations. Strolling through the fort, I noticed various military dress on display. They looked like they had stepped out of a Hollywood set – the riders with their whiskers, elaborate mustaches, and colorful headscarves. I was waiting for the Bengal Lancers or Errol Flynn to appear.

Sufficiently drenched, I phoned the driver to meet me out front where the masses were idling, selling trinkets, or waiting for something to happen. As the lone white man, I passed through the crowd unnoticed, almost trying to hold off just about everyone selling or wanting something. One very eager "salesman" followed me, determined I would eventually succumb and rent an "Indian helicopter" – an open-air contraption for two.

Once I made it to the car, we proceeded in the general direction of the ancient mosque *Jama Masjid,* completed in 1656, and it is a tremendously impressive structure. I made a quick stop, not wanting to repeat the exercise of having to find my driver. From the mosque, we cut through "old Delhi," or as my driver said, with a nervous laugh, "Welcome to Pakistan." He may not have been that far off.

Old Delhi looks like the pics we've all seen, at one time or another, of the old sections of Kabul, Karachi, or Dacca. There are still many Muslims in this part of town; streets (loose definition) are jammed with everything that can be used to move from point A to point B, including animals. The electric wires running along the side of shops and homes were, for the most part, enormous, tangled masses of electrical wire. It was clear that Verizon had not made any recent service calls to old Delhi!

As we slowly walked through the old neighborhood, over the ruts, rising to one side and down the other, I could picture the perfect Hollywood movie scene placing our valiant American agent searching for his contact in one side alley or another. Would he find him alive or stabbed? Perhaps the Homeland series needed a sequel.

Our next stop was the *Humayun's* Tomb – not quite as old as the *Taj Mahal* but quite magnificent. When you can't see anymore through the sweat running down your face, it's time to move on and retreat to your car. My tour concluded with a visit to the Gandhi Museum. I found it impressive, if for nothing else, because of its simplicity when compared to one man's undeniably remarkable achievements and the mark he left on India. By the way, if you have not seen the movie *Gandhi*, it's a winner, again and again.

I've been thinking, and usually, when that happens, I lie down for a few minutes, and the urge disappears. I suppose I may have seemed harsh in describing Delhi. After all, this city is political. Having lived and worked in Washington, D.C., I could see there were more than just a few similarities between capitals. In Delhi, the principal architectural focus is the India Gate on one end of the *Rajpath*, and on the other is *Rashtrapati Bjavan*, or Government House, the seat of power in India. The design is wonderfully achieved and reminded me of that stretch of road from Capitol Hill to the White House. Delhi is swarming with people of all political stripes, all of whom want "access" or seek to provide a means of influencing the course of political events in Delhi. As a political city, Washington DC crawls with lobbyists of all stripes, seeking special access to influence Congress or the Executive Branch. Granted, some of these characters bring their unique brand of sleaze with enough to go around several times over.

A few words about the "Diplomatic Enclave." My hotel was in a relatively nice area of town, given everything I'd seen thus far. As I have mentioned before, in the Enclave, there is a different feel as it is home to diplomatic missions ministers and dignitaries.

I should note that it's not unusual to see the occasional Bentley whizzing past those pesky chimps, or staff officer cars from various military branches.

My bags are packed, and I have arranged for a driver to take me to Indira Gandhi International Airport. Tomorrow, I have an early flight to Hyderabad.

Delhi – Monsoon season

HYDERABAD

A Tale of Two Cities

"The city of dreams, the city of mystery, and the city that never sleeps."

elcome to Hyderabad City, the capital of Hyderabad State, with a majority Muslim population. It is a tale of two cities-one of glitter and gold, the other of poverty, poor infrastructure, and swarming crowds. My hotel, the MindSpace, left no room for misunderstanding that I was at the epicenter of the IT business in India. Here you will find a couple of square miles devoted solely to the business of IT, and every US corporate logo is in full view, including my good friends at Verizon. I thought I should try to find my very friendly customer service representative known to me only as "Hi, I'm Mike from Verizon, your tier 1 support specialist." I would tell "Mike", as I have time and time again, that I am still having problems with my internet connectivity;

"No problem Mr. Richard I will fix it completely; tell me, is your computer plugged in?"

During my short stay here, I've bumped into young techs from Russia, China, cool dudes from the US, and tons of Indian software developers. This is a crowd that seems to move in packs; you see them in the buffet restaurants, all sitting at the same table and enjoying their lunch and most certainly discussing perplexing code problems or maybe how to handle those insistent, obnoxious customers, especially those from the US, who never cease to complain about their internet.

For those poor little ex-pats away from home, my hotel has done everything possible to pamper them, from ethnic restaurants, bars, 24-hour food and alcohol service, and room service. There are plenty of little nooks and crannies where they can hide from others and ponder their screens late into the night. An

Olympic pool and plush suites ensure comfort. This is a secret society, dude, not open to just anyone.

I was greeted warmly by my customer in Hyderabad.
The weather here is a lovely 115 degrees.

My clients are in a three-story building in a part of Hyderabad, inconsistent with MindSpace and IT Nirvana, shall we say? It's the real Hyderabad, the one resembling Delhi I've seen. While the traffic here is horrendous, it is not hideously bad as in Delhi. Here traffic moves. I did see a few water buffaloes meandering along the medium, not the least perturbed by traffic. It is hot in Hyderabad but not oven-like as in Delhi, and the humidity is bearable, meaning less lethal.

As I entered the building, the receptionist handed me a large bouquet. Lovely, but what do I do with them? Carry them around their office. Admittedly, I was at a loss for what to do, then smiled and put them on the counter, promising to recoup them when I left. Here, one is almost a rock star turning heads, big smiles all around as if I was a guru, or yes, that special rock star.

We met briefly with the Managing Director, but only after first taking off our shoes. Lace shoes? What was I thinking? I padded around in a pair of slippers, not exactly the look I was trying to convey.

I have had my share of Indian buffet lunches and dinners, yet I am making a point of dining with the Managing Director and his wife tonight. After that, I should think I will have met my Indian food quota or even surpassed it. No more green sauces, lamb, chicken, or seafood, and thank you, and I will hold off with the yogurt concoctions, the vegetables simmering in a pale green sauce, and the flatbread. Enough of the endless and, yes, delicious sugary desserts. For now, enough of it all. Please.

The Managing Director and his lovely wife picked me up at my hotel. I felt underdressed with him in a snappy suit and she in a beautiful, colorful sari. We drove through the rush hour madhouse to a lovely hotel and a restaurant which was going to be, as I suspected, a full buffet with a complete line of curries and soups on the one side and an entire display of vegetarian dishes on the other. There was a little section for appetizers (snacks are how appetizers are referred to), a large table with multiple cakes, ice cream (mango was delicious), sweet Indian specialties, and more. I'd been through enough buffets, so I knew the drill and picked up my plate and took this or that depending on the look or if my host/hostess suggested I try something I'd never seen in my entire life; then I took the plunge and prayed.

All in all, a wonderful dinner, and we took the opportunity to learn a little about one another. I told them I would most likely returning to Hyderabad several more times. Yes, business was progressing. They seemed delighted. I knew my host and hostess were the product of an arranged marriage. I told them I was no longer entangled in a marriage. They told me their daughter, on the West Coast in San Francisco, is a chemical engineer (surprise!), and they are hopeful there will be an eventual arranged marriage. I probably would not hold my breath on that one.

Back at my hotel, I repacked my suitcase, something I could do with my eyes closed. Tomorrow, I leave for Mumbai. Hang on!

MUMBAI

(Formerly Known as Bombay)

Five Sketch Stories

BACK BAY: THE QUEEN'S NECKLACE

"The heart of India beats in Mumbai."

Mumbai is a sprawling city of 27 million people, and 4 million or so live in slums.

In his best Hinglish (English and Hindi), my cab driver explained that we were on a section of Marine Drive known as the

Queen's Necklace. I had to play tourist, so I asked why it was called that. He looked at me from his rearview mirror and smiled, a smile that said, "Soooo, first time in Mumbai? Got a live one here!" You knew it, and he knew it—a first-timer.

If viewed at night and ideally from an elevated vantage point anywhere along the drive, the streetlights that hug the road along Back Bay resemble a string of pearls, as in a necklace. Her Majesty, God bless her, would have been pleased. I took this story, like so many others, at face value. I always enjoy visiting the venerable Taj Palace Hotel for its over-the-top hospitality and the colorful route one enjoys getting there. Like most traffic anywhere in India, especially in this part of Mumbai, traffic is more congested. The roads twist and turn, making for a lively ride. One eventually gets used to this mix of cars, tuk-tuks, bicycles, motorbikes, and anything else that could serve as a mode of transportation. I recall seeing a man driving a motorbike with his wife on the back and his daughter squashed between the two. At the front of the bike was a half-naked baby happily sitting in the very front basket. The Taj, that majesty of all hotels, is tucked between *B.K. Boman Behram Marg* and *P.J. Ramchandani Marg*. Either way, it's not like you will miss it. I would dare say that every cab driver in Mumbai, worth his salt, knows the Taj and its history.

Once my bags were scanned and cleared at the Taj, I entered a little Heaven, where service was impeccable. In the lobby, I was greeted with a *Tulsi* necklace, believed to bring health and peace; a *bindi* (a red dot) was placed on my forehead to symbolize health and happiness. The Taj's service is so outstanding that you can stand anywhere in the lobby and within seconds staff will approach you to ask if you need help. The fact that a hotel guest might be the slightest unsure about something cannot be tolerated. They must be assisted in all manner possible. What we in the USA might consider as service so entirely over the top, the Taj believes it's only a good start. It's a beautiful place to stay, the restaurants are magnificent, and having breakfast, along the elegant passageway, by the pool is a lovely way to start the day.

THE HARBOUR BAR, TAJ HOTEL

*I*f you are looking for a casual yet sophisticated place to spend some time with a cold drink, I suggest you take a cab to the Taj Palace. You can hang out for a few drinks at Harbour Bar. Guarantee you will see quite a collection of people, some looking like they stepped out of a fashion magazine, others shall we say, scream "Yankee" in their eclectic attire and their need to speak loudly enough to find another lonely ex-pat American with whom they could feel at home or commiserate with and discuss the latest football games.

I usually steer clear of my fellow ex-pats. If it's a place known to be frequented by Americans, you won't find me there. Sorry, but travelling overseas I don't like to cluster with Americans, something about a target on my back. That's the truth. I am guilty of not even following a home sports team, the standard icebreaker for all Americans. Not me, not interested, and I make no apologies. At the bar, I took the opportunity to chat with the bartender. I enjoy digging for a little local lore, some unique perspective, and perhaps even finding a lead on a possible story. On my second gin, I broached the topic of the Taj attack and siege by the terrorists on 26 November 2008. The attack had been carefully organized by ten members of Lashkar-e-Taiba, an Islamic militant organization based in Pakistan. A total of 175 people died, including nine attackers, and more than 300 were wounded. The barkeep rested his arm on the highly polished bar; he thought for a moment, then recounted that it was his day off when the attack occurred! I wondered, how do you say one lucky guy in Hindi? He recalled gathering around the television and watching in horror the tragic events of that day. When the smoke had cleared, he returned to the Taj to offer his help. He told me he remembered seeing bodies lined up in the hallway and recognizing many of them as his friends and colleagues.

I promised him I would return the next day for lunch. I did, sitting by the window looking towards the water, the Gateway of India, and the assembly of decorated little water taxis ready for a trip to Elephant Island. Another steamy day was building in Mumbai.

Billionaire Row in India's Mumbai

Every time I have been to Mumbai, drivers, taxi drivers, or anyone behind the wheel is fond of pointing out interesting landmarks. In a vast and sprawling city such as Mumbai, arguably with some of the biggest slums in the world, even the making of a well-known movie might well be a factoid of interest. But it's not. Bad for tourism.

As you navigate through massive congestion, your driver will most likely note, "And on your right, sir, is India's most expensive residence." That's right; the 400,000-square-foot property is worth $1-2 billion. That would be in dollars, not rupees. This spacious tiny home of 400,000 square feet includes 27 stories, six dedicated to cars. This unassuming real estate sits squarely in Mumbai on Altamont Road, also known as India's Billionaire Row. Let me tell you, the locals love showing it off, including my cab driver.

An Unforgettable Indian Birthday Dinner

Just my luck, I should celebrate my birthday in Mumbai. My customer suggested another hotel for drinks and dinner. Lovely idea and I took a cab arriving early to check out the over-the-top lounge area, where everything from chandeliers to attentive and attractive servers was stunning. My customer and his wife arrived, and we were ushered into a private room for drinks. There was good air conditioning, and in Mumbai, where the humidity usually beats the temperature by a country mile, AC is a necessity; otherwise, your clothes slowly rot. Trust me on this. I emphasize this because the heat and humidity are a force to be reconned with. The dining room was barely occupied, so the staff felt they needed to do something, and they did. Drinks, bottled water, wine lists, appetizers, and main courses arrived with military precision. We drank enough wine to pickle ourselves silly. Having given us enough room to breathe and to drink some more, a cart was wheeled to our table. On the cart was a giant chocolate cake with enough candles to convey that I was not celebrating my fifteenth birthday. The wait staff appeared, standing in a semi-circle and sand Happy Birthday, "Mister." Beautifully done; we clapped, I cut the cake, and we each ate a piece. I then asked that the remainder of the cake be shared with the staff. The final touch of perfection was the manager placing a sampler of three single malt Scotch in front of me. Most delicately done and in a beautiful manner.

THE GATEWAY TO INDIA

$\mathcal{A}$rguably the most significant monument in Mumbai is the Gateway of India. It has been called the Taj Mahal of Mumbai. Like so many things in India, the Gateway has its fascinating and haunting history. If the Gateway could speak, what tales would it tell? It was constructed to commemorate the 1911 royal visit to Mumbai (Bombay) of King George V and Queen Mary and was completed in December 1924. At the time, it served as the ceremonial entry point for high-ranking British officials. In an irony of history, the First Battalion of the Somerset Light Infantry were the last British troops to leave India, passing smartly through the arches on February 28, 1948. The British had left India once and for all. It was a historic moment and, for all of India, a moment to savor, indeed.

I recalled one of my many sleepless nights in India due in part, I suspect, to my system trying to adjust from three or more different time zones, having left another country somewhere in the world, the Middle East, or Latin America perhaps. I was a zombie stepping over continents. In the wee morning hours, I would stand out on my small screened-in porch, perhaps more of a galley way, really, no more than five feet wide, and observe my world and the Gateway of India in all its mysterious glory. The cacophony of noise from cars, trucks, and tuk-tuks honking horns would soon come, but at four in the morning, it was quiet but already hot, and the humidity was rising.

It was impossible to escape the smell of Mumbai, that mix of salty humid air combined with sea and sweat, as well as the scent of incense and charcoal. Everything stood still; the brightly painted boats barely moved on the water. Soon they would be shuttle tourists to and from Elephant Island, the City of Caves in the Sea of Oman.

I repacked my suitcase and checked out. Madras awaited me, or should I say Chennai?

CHENNAI

By Kartshutterarts – Own work

"There is a lovely church in Madras, India, with a monument to a British army officer eaten by a tiger. It simply says: 'Eaten by a tiger.' Let's face it, no matter how much we try, none of us will get an epitaph as good as that." Unknown

Chennai, formerly known as Madras, is the capital city of Tamil Nadu and is known as the Gateway to South India. If you look at your map of India, you will see that it is the southernmost Indian state. My stay in Chennai was all about business. It was short but long enough for me to love Chennai and the beautiful Coromandel Coast of the Bay of Bengal. I made sure I appreciated some of the incredible seafood dishes known from this coastal region.

My customer told me he wanted to take us to a commercial area near the hotel and introduce us to an up-and-coming new restaurant, considered one of the trendiest restaurants in Chennai. In other words, an excellent place to go and be seen by the up-and-coming, entrepreneurial crowd in Chennai.

I appreciated the gesture, not knowing precisely what he had in mind, but how could I resist?

Once there, he ordered a selection of "snacks," the Indian version of appetizers, spicy dips, and cold beers, which helped things along. All were very thoughtful, and the gesture was much appreciated. Just before leaving, he asked that we all remain seated then the restaurant manager brought out a beautiful cake-like dessert with a "Welcome to Chennai" written out in icing. It was a wonderful and thoughtful gesture.

It's one of those many places in India I have jotted down as a "must return." It's a growing list.

Tomorrow, I fly north to Kolkata, formerly known as Calcutta.

KOLKATA

(Formerly known as Calcutta)

GREAT PLANS OF MICE AND MEN

*L*et me give you a quick overview. Kolkata is the capital of West Bengal and is located approximately 50 miles west of Bangladesh. My colleague and I arrived late in the afternoon, the day before our series of meetings, including a briefing on agricultural issues and how our suite of business services might add value. I knew it was an ambitious agenda, but I remained determined. Yet, while I wanted to maximize my stay on the ground in India, I did not relish the idea of returning home more dead than alive. I was excited and optimistic and hoped to conclude my meetings quickly. I had a driver lined up and a personal agenda that would let me see some of the sites of this fantastic city.

We arrived at our hotel and unpacked for the umpteenth time, or so it seemed. I can pack and unpack in my sleep and not miss a beat. That evening we had a grand dinner and enjoyed ourselves as this was the last stop on our great India tour. We were still alive. The business had been concluded swiftly and efficiently, and we had made excellent progress.

The nature of this business

Let's suppose you have little or no experience conducting business in developing countries such as Vietnam, India, Indonesia, or other similar countries. In that case, it's imperative that you understand the importance of country customs. It's perhaps not as important as striking a deal, but it's so easy to lose face by ignoring their business customs. The role of time, for example, in conducting business is vital. I have met many business compatriots who believe that one flies into country A, attends a dinner meeting and a working breakfast, only to leave a few hours later presuming that business will magically happen. As Americans, our business concept often differs from the reality and process in many developing countries. We want action now, but it does not work that way. Sorry to burst your bubble. I can think of many examples of getting to know a company CEO, social dinners, sometimes with the spouse, having dinner with the family at a restaurant, or celebrating his wife's birthday with their employees. These are my examples, of course, but something to think about as you carve out your own way.

Offshore business is often conducted sequentially over time, with each visit building a stronger rapport than the previous one. As many mistakenly believe, it is not a question of planting the flag on Indian soil and expecting business to drop at our feet as if it were an Amazon delivery. I have conducted business and built relationships in over twenty-five countries. Traveling to India, as an example, is, at the very minimum, at least a two-to three-time annual event and a minimum stay of a week or more all over a period of several years. If you are seriously thinking about opening a business storefront, then, that's a different story entirely. That action says you are there to stay and committed to doing business over the long haul. It sends a powerful message. For a small company, it's a complex and financially steep challenge.

Delhi-belly

Just before our last dinner, the night before our return home, the infamous "Delhi-belly," a stomach flu variation that shows no remorse, hit me with the force of a two-by-four. I had felt confident, maybe even a bit cocky, at successfully dodging the Indian bullet. Now I was facing an onslaught of chills and fever. I could not keep anything down. I was a mess. The thought of leaving my room and taking a tourist cab ride anywhere struck fear in me. In the back of my mind, the departure clock ticked loudly and relentlessly. We had a flight out that following afternoon to Dubai, then a connecting flight to Washington, Dulles. International schedules do not re-arrange themselves to suit someone's needs. Anyone who has flown 14–16 hour stretches knows how miserable it can be to be sick thousands of miles away from your bed.

In my hotel room, I emptied my kit bag of every possible medicine that might work. Anything. I was a desperate man, a man on a mission. Simply put, I wanted to leave the country as fast as possible. Pale-faced, weak, sleepless, dehydrated, and gaunt, I clutched my suitcase handle for dear life and proceeded to check out. The hotel manager who had heard about my situation, likely from my colleague, handed me a mixture in a baggie, assuring me that it would work miracles. Does a drowning man refuse a life preserver? I took it with hope and a silent prayer. Eventually, it worked insofar as bringing me down from a 5-Alarm to a slightly more manageable 3-Alarm level. Nothing is perfect. I found a pharmacy at the airport, and they suggested a multi-potion mix (two of A every hour and 1 of B every hour, and 1 of C…). I took them as directed and prayed. It reminded me of a similar situation in Hanoi. I felt as if I was near death. Such fun.

Some twenty-plus hours later, with a stopover in Dubai, I landed at Washington Dulles International Airport and a familiar DHS greeting, "Welcome Home, sir," as I sailed through customs. I was only a slightly improved version of my former self: weak and far from perfect but a grateful man.

SELECTED RECIPES

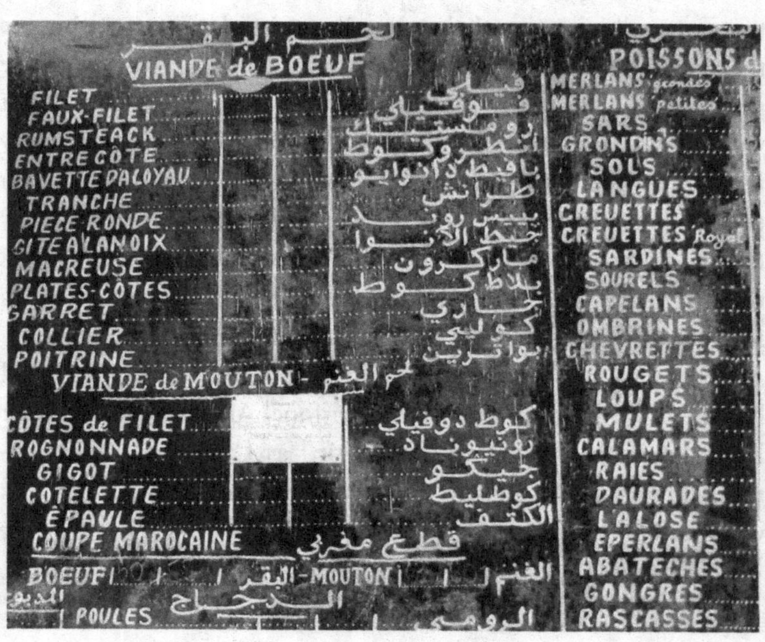

VIETNAM

Hanoi in monsoon season

CARAMELIZED CHICKEN
OR GA KHO

I found this exciting recipe while searching for different food experiences in Hanoi. I dodged in and out of the old quarter and sought cover from the sudden monsoon downpours. I didn't have to go far to find what I wanted. A busy side street and an even more active vendor. It was spicy, but there was always Hanoi beer to cool the fire. To tell you God's truth, what struck me about this dish was the intriguing mix of ingredients, from rice vinegar and fish sauce to ginger, garlic, and Thai chili.

I found myself in total heaven, and that's the main reason why I am presenting this recipe today, along with some delicious French wines, of course. Let's be sensible. I hope you enjoy it.

Caramelized Chicken – Ga Kho
(Adapted from *Food Wishes*)

Ingredients
2.5 lbs. chicken thigh
3/4 cup brown sugar
1/3 cup fish sauce
1/3 cup rice vinegar

1/3 cup water

Four cloves of crushed garlic

2 tbsp chopped ginger (you can also substitute finely minced lemongrass)

Two shallots minced

2 tbsp fish sauce for the marinade

1 tbsp brown sugar for the marinade

Two jalapenos or 1 Thai chili (optional, but yes!) thinly sliced

Two green onions, sliced about 1/2 inch

Fresh cracked pepper

Roasted sesame (optional) or roasted peanuts.

2 tbsp cooking oil

Directions

Marinade the chicken with two tbs of fish sauce and one tbs brown sugar for about 1/2 hr.

Then, with a glass of chilled white Burgundy in one hand, make the sauce; with the other hand, combine 3/4 cup brown sugar, 1/3 cup water, rice vinegar, and fish sauce and mix in a small bowl until dissolved. Add the ginger, shallots, and garlic and set aside.

Heat a large pan on high with cooking oil and add the chicken with the flat surface of the thigh facing down. Allow them to sear without touching them for a minute, then pour about 1/4 of the sauce. Do not move the chicken around; you want it to sear and caramelize. The sauce will thicken, and the chicken will brown after a few minutes.

Check to see if it's nicely caramelized, then turn the chicken pieces over and pour in the rest of the sauce. Continue to cook until the sauce is reduced to a nice thick consistency, and just as you turn off the heat, toss in the chilies and green onions. Transfer to a serving platter and generously top with roasted sesame, freshly cracked pepper, and a freshly sliced baguette.

Now about those wines...

It makes perfect sense to pair French wines with this spicy dish. I favor an excellent selection of white wines from Burgundy, the Loire, and Rhone Valley, and finally, a little Rose from Provence, of course! Decisions – decisions.

Domaine Sainte Claire Saint-Bris J.M. Brocard

Burgundy, France

100% Sauvignon Blanc

This is a classic example of a high-toned and citrusy Sauvignon Blanc. And it's good. The finish is clean and snappy, in other words, a great summertime wine (even better if you are in the tropics and like the rain and steamy weather! It worked for me.)

Domaine de la Fouquette, Rose d'Aurore

Provence, France

65% Grenache/30% Cinsault/5% Rolle

The color of this wine is immediately captivating, with a spectrum of pale salmon, pale pink, and silvery watermelon in the glass—a truly stunning Rose. Buy it by the case, please!

Saigon by night

Ho Chi Minh City, once known as Saigon (and often still is unless you are dealing with the government), was once known as 'the Paris of the Orient.' Not too difficult to imagine why. It is a city of broad boulevards with French architecture everywhere. You can throw a croissant in any direction and hit someone who speaks French. The link to French-influenced food is equally apparent, from baguettes, *croissants,* and *petit pain au chocolat* (croissants re-imagined with chocolate filling) to the flan or custard tarts.

And that's only the beginning. From grilled chicken, beef *Luc Lac,* and numerous pork dishes to a wide variety of succulent seafood prepared in many ways; it is easy to wrap one's arms around this cuisine now and forever. Today, Saigon is a vibrant city pulsating with economic activity. You can feel the energy; it is moving toward its destiny and can't get there fast enough. High-end boutiques with exclusive brand names jockey for a more favorable position on the avenues next to inviting restaurants with exotic names. You cannot hide or avoid the obvious; this city pulsates!

Vietnamese Grilled Chicken with Lemongrass or Ga Nuong Xa

Ingredients
3-lbs chicken drumsticks, or whichever part of the chicken you like
Two lemongrass stalks, finely minced
Four cloves of garlic

2-inch knob of ginger
1 tbsp *Nuoc Mam* (Vietnamese Fish Sauce), or to taste (will accept substitutes)
1 tbsp brown sugar, or to taste
1 tsp salt, or to taste
1 tsp ground black pepper, or to taste

Directions:

Grind lemongrass*, garlic, and ginger in a food processor until finely minced.

Peel away the top layers of the lemongrass until you get to the softer, fleshier part -that yellow-pale stalk that is easy to slice; make sure you cut off the bulb; make thin slices up to 2/3 of the stem; pound it or put it in a processor for a whirl. It should now be ready to use in your recipe.

Add fish sauce, salt, ground black pepper, and brown sugar. Taste and adjust seasonings if necessary.

Add chicken and mix in marinade thoroughly. Allow to chill in the fridge for an hour—Grill baby grill.

Enjoy with rice and grilled vegetables, fresh salad, and for dessert, mango ice cream.

Of beer, wine, and other things critical

I would forgo wine with this dish and order an ice-cold Saigon beer instead. They keep them in the back. Ask, delicately, if they have any Hanoi beer, try it, compare it, and let me know your favorite. If they sneer at you, then it wasn't a good idea. Maybe they serve dog; who knows! If some of your guests are pouting and insisting on wine, one option is always to ask them to leave.

Another option would have them enjoy the steep view from your patio, then push them off (it's only an option, OK?). The more polite option (if pressed) would be to suggest a chilled New Zealand *Sauvignon Blanc* or a *Rose de Provence.* Either one should keep them happy and quiet. *Merci.*

TURKEY

Istanbul -European side

LOBSTER GREEN CURRY
OR *ISTAKOZ* CURRY

I may have tweaked the recipe here and there, but I have maintained the overall integrity of the recipe. Two giant lobsters should feed four. It might be difficult to get more than that into a pan. Invite your friends for your first annual lobster race. Always fun!

Ingredients

For the green curry paste:
Four green chilies and seeds were removed.
Three lemongrass sticks are finely chopped.
Four cloves of garlic, peeled.
One piece galangal, equivalent to a teaspoon chopped (ginger can be used instead)
2 tsp black peppercorns
1 tsp shrimp paste
Four kaffir lime leaves
1 tbsp fish sauce
One bunch of coriander, stalks included.

For lobsters:

Two angry lobsters both demanding justice and equal rights (naturally) 750g- 800g each
One onion
One red chili
Three lime leaves
400 ml coconut milk
Two limes
Three tablespoons roughly chopped coriander.

Preparation

First, one must start with a shot of Turkish 'raki.' This is a critical step in ensuring you have a wonderful meal.

Make the curry paste with a mortar and pestle, or use your food processor. It makes no difference to me, but if Big Brother is watching, it's a different story.) Pound or blend all the ingredients to create a paste. You can store the paste in the fridge for up to a week. Some people do. I would most likely forget about it until it developed a life.

If you plan on terminating your lobster at home, with extreme prejudice, use the following method: While cursing its mother, insert a large and heavy cook's knife into the middle of the lobster's head in the same direction as its body and bring it down sharply in a guillotine action to split it in half. Turn the lobster 180 degrees and repeat the step to cleave the lobster entirely in half.

Despite any post-mortem twitching, your lobster will now be quite dead. Remove the hard stomach sac in the head and repeat the process for the second lobster. Now remove the bands from the lobsters' claws; crack the large claws with the back of the knife so that they will cook quicker and be easier to negotiate when eating.

After witnessing your death in the afternoon, I would suggest that another shot of 'raki' is probably in order.

Heat a large sauté pan with a coating of oil. Place the lobsters in the pan, cut side down, and leave for a few minutes to seal the tail meat and the coral. Turn the lobsters and color the shells before removing them. The lobsters should still be raw in the middle.

Add a little more oil without washing the pan. Peel and chop the onion and stew it gently for 4-5 minutes.

Once softened, add the red chili, very finely sliced, the finely shredded lime leaves, and then four tablespoons of the curry paste with a generous pinch of salt. Stir well, then pour in the coconut milk and bring to a boil.

Place the lobsters, shell side down, into the sauce, cover with grease-proof paper, and let them poach gently in the sauce for 4-5 minutes. Don't let the sauce boil — if you do, the meat will toughen.

Taste the sauce for seasoning — it may need a little more chili flake if it's not sufficiently hot for you — and then sharpen the taste with the juice of the two limes. Sprinkle with the chopped coriander. Serve with boiled rice, lobster crackers, picks (for the lobsters only), and several napkins.

Now about those wines

Anfora (Pamukkale) Sauvignon Blanc

Kavaklidere Angora White Wine

Urla Chardonnay (I can personally vouch for this from a wonderful winery I visited in southern Turkey, near Izmir.)

Yeni Raki (as an aperitif, digestif, rubdown, or for any occasion with friends). Say it with me, "It's always time for Raki."

Turkish Fried Calamari

*K*alamar or Calamari (squid) is the most loved seafood in Turkey. Yes, even if they do beat the living daylights out of them. But it's only for their good and ours. Poisoning is just so passe.

Ingredients

6 Squid tubes (fresh and cleaned) ring cut 1-in/1-in
Two teaspoons of sugar
Four teaspoons of baking soda
One teaspoon salt
2 cups vegetable oil
2 cups of flour

Instructions

Put the flour into a bowl and dip the Calamari rings into the flour individually. Make sure all Calamari rings are covered with flour.

Pour the vegetable oil into a deep-frying pan and heat the vegetable oil. You can quickly tell if the oil is sufficiently heated by sprinkling some flour on the oil. If you see the flour sizzling, then go ahead and drop in the calamari rings.

Place a paper towel onto a serving plate to remove the excess vegetable oil from the top of the calamari rings.

Once the calamari rings get golden, take them out with the skimmer spoon and place them on the paper toweled serving plate.

Serve.

Now, about those wines

I am going out on a proverbial limb by saying that almost any crisp, citrussy white wine would work magically, which means Sauvignon Blanc would be the obvious choice. I am an equal-opportunity wine enthusiast, so plenty of other French, Italian, Spanish, and Portuguese whites would qualify just as well. I would add *Picpoul* (one of my favorites, from the Languedoc region in the South of France; it pairs almost naturally, one might say with seafood. Pick up the case, you won't be sorry) Alberino, Chablis, and Vinho Verde are all squid friendly.

MOROCCO

Casablanca trailer

MOROCCAN CHICKEN OR
POULET À LA MAROCAINE

Adapted in part from Saveur Magazine

Ingredients

Six boneless skin-on chicken breasts pounded 3⁄4" thick.

16 Tbsp. Extra-virgin olive oil

Kosher salt and freshly ground black pepper, to taste

4 cups chicken broth

2 lbs. Carrots cut into 1⁄4" rounds.

One large white onion, minced

1 1⁄2 cups fresh orange juice

4 Tbsp. Unsalted butter

Two peeled oranges, segmented

3⁄4 cup plus 2 tsp. *Harissa**

2 tsp. Sherry vinegar

3 oz. Dandelion greens

3⁄4 cup pitted oil-cured black olives, roughly chopped

Two shallots, thinly sliced

Preparation

Put the chicken in a dish; drizzle with 3 tbsp. Oil; season with salt and pepper. Set it aside. Bring broth to a boil in a 6-qt—Pan over medium-high heat.

Add carrots; cook until tender, 15–20 minutes. Drain. Heat 1/2 cup Oil in a 4-qt. Pot over high heat. Add onions; cook until soft, 4–5 minutes.

Or, add carrots; cook for 6–8 minutes. *Purée* in a food processor with 2 tbsp. Oil.

Season with salt and pepper; keep warm.

Heat orange juice in a 2-quart saucepan over medium-high heat. Cook until reduced by half, 12–15 minutes. Whisk in butter, season with salt and pepper. Add orange segments; set the sauce aside.

Heat oven to 400°. Heat a grill pan over medium-high heat. Working in 3 batches, add chicken, skin side down; cook until crisp, 8–10 minutes. Transfer chicken, skin side up, to a baking sheet. Brush with 3/4 cup *harissa*. Bake until cooked, 6–8 minutes.

Whisk together the remaining oil and harissa in a bowl with the sherry vinegar. Add greens, olives, and shallots, and toss. Divide carrot *purée* between 6 plates: top each with salad and a chicken breast—spoon sauce over each.

(Serves 6)

*Harissa
3-4 dried ancho chilies
3-4 garlic cloves, chopped
One teaspoon cumin
One teaspoon coriander
One teaspoon of caraway seed
1/2 teaspoon salt
1/2 cup olive oil
Two tablespoons water

Stem and de-seed chilies. Tear them into rough pieces, place them in a jar, and cover them with hot water. Let them soak for about an hour (wine time), then drain and pat dry.

Transfer them to a food processor and add garlic, spices, and salt. Blend until the mixture is a coarse paste; then add olive oil and water and blend until smooth.

Serving suggestions: A traditional cucumber and tomato Arabic salad. A mixture or single type of cured olives, including spicy olives (my favorite). Lastly, a simple green salad with olive oil, French wine vinegar, and Dijon mustard. Yum!

Now about those wines...
Catena Chardonnay, Mendoza, Argentina

Chateau de la *Tuilerie*, *Costieres de* Nimes, France Cotes du Rhône Blanc, France

Halana Syrah Rose is a robust wine with hints of rose petals and strawberries—a Moroccan intrigue.

LEBANON

Beirut: Photo by Karan Jain USA
Ferris Wheel and the Corniche, CC BY-SA 2.0,

Tabouleh Salad

Ingredients
½ cup refined bulgur wheat
Four firm Roma tomatoes, very finely chopped.
1 English cucumber (hothouse cucumber, preferably with an English accent) very finely chopped.
Two bunches of parsley, part of the stems removed, washed and well-dried, and finely chopped.
12-15 fresh mint leaves, stems removed, cleaned, well-dried, very finely chopped.
Four green onions, white and green parts, very finely chopped.
Salt
3-4 tablespoons lime juice (lemon juice, if you prefer)
3-4 tablespoons extra-virgin olive oil

Directions
Fold the ingredients together, making sure all ingredients are well mixed together.

Romaine lettuce leaves to serve, optional.

The finer you chop the vegetables, the better. Remember not to chop your fingers in the process.

To serve a smaller crowd, cut the recipe in half.

You can refrigerate tabouli in a tight-lid container for two days or so. It's important to try and drain some of the juice out before refrigerating leftover tabouli.

DEMOCRATIC REPUBLIC OF CONGO

As you ease into the Congo experience, I have included a couple of exciting dishes for you to consider and help pave your way, perhaps, into your own heart of darkness. Why did I choose seemingly basic staples like chicken, papaya, and rice? Those simple ingredients were almost a staple of our lunch or dinner. Of course, to mix things up and go wild, bananas, mangoes, or pineapples would be added to the mystery meat, along with rice, the staple of any third-world country. Manioc dishes were occasionally offered. The operative word, of course, was "offered." Maybe by adding this dish, I am putting those "food basics" to bed once and for all.

Papaya Chicken /
Poulet Au Papaya

*(This recipe is taken, in part, from
La Cuisine Coloniale)*

Ingredients

1/2 teaspoon salt

1/4 teaspoon cayenne pepper (please feel free to use *pili-pili* if you have it but use it judiciously.)

One tablespoon of lime juice

Two whole chickens were cut up and skinned to an inch of their lives.

Three tablespoons cornstarch

Three tablespoons of chicken broth

1/4 cup finely chopped onion

Two tablespoons oil

One tablespoon of peeled – minced ginger root

1 1/2 cups chicken broth

1 medium green bell pepper – cut into 1 1/2 inch

1 papaya, peeled, seeded – cut into 2 x 5/8 in strips

2 cups hot cooked rice

Directions

In a medium bowl, combine salt, cayenne, and lime juice. Stir in chicken pieces to coat.

In a small bowl, combine cornstarch and three tablespoons of chicken broth.

Set aside. In a large skillet over medium-high heat, cook onion in oil until crisp-tender.

Add chicken mixture and ginger root; stir fry until chicken is no longer pink.

Add 1 1/2 cups chicken broth; bring to a boil. Reduce heat; simmer for 2 minutes.

Add green peppers; cook for 2 minutes or until crisp and tender. Add papaya strips; stir in the cornstarch mixture.

Cook and stir until thickened, and papaya is heated through. Serve over hot cooked rice.

While at the dinner table, the rice would be brought by either Albert or Emanuel, each one sporting a white serving jacket, looking quite dapper even in their shorts and bare feet.

Now about those wines

I am mixing the heart of Africa with South African, French, and California wines. What a way to go!

Newton Red Label Chardonnay *Sonoma, Napa, California*
I take my hat off to this little gem. Aromas of white nectarine and vanilla spice, together with baked apple and caramel notes, carry through to the palate, where they are accented by ripe melon and fresh pineapple flavors.

Chateau *Puycastaing* White Graves *Bordeaux, France*

A blend of 80% Semillon and 20% Sauvignon Blanc shows the aromas of acacia flowers, lemon curd, box tree, and exotic fruits.

A nicely chilled Primus Beer. Quite simply an exceptional choice, and you will fit right in!

CHICKEN IN PEANUT SAUCE -CONGO-STYLE

Poulet à la Muambe

(Adapte in part from Les Aventures de Jamie & Katie)

The Chicken in Peanut Sauce dish is something of a tribute to those hot, humid evenings when ex-pats of various nationalities would gather for news and engage in friendly conversations over a local beer, a hot dish, or maybe even a *Dame Blanche* ice cream for dessert and take in a view of their world, Kinshasa, the mighty Congo River, perhaps even a picture of Brazzaville across the river. And the vastness that lay beyond somewhere, deep in the "bush."

Ingredients

Chicken
One whole chicken cut up
1 t salt
a few dashes of ground ginger
1/2 cup green onion (chopped)
1/2 stalk of celery (chopped)

Bay leaf
One small white onion (chopped)
Eight cloves of garlic (crushed and chopped)
Vegetable oil

Sauce
Two big tomatoes
One small onion
1/2 cup green onion
1/2 stalk of celery
One big green bell pepper
One small eggplant
1/2 cup water
1/3-1/2 cup all-natural peanut butter, depending on taste *(I used a fine local varietal -crunchy PB, and it worked great)*
1/2 t salt
1-3 small chili peppers (chopped or whole), depending on taste (in order of increasing spiciness: Jalapeño, Fresno, Serrano, or Thai chili peppers would work well)

Directions
Prepare the chicken.

Cut the whole chicken into quarters or pieces. Cut small gashes in the meat and rub it with ground ginger.

Put chicken in a large pot and season with salt, ginger, green onions, celery, bay leaf, onion, and garlic.

Cook for 10 minutes on medium heat, flipping the chicken pieces once. Remove the chicken and set aside the remaining juice and cooked vegetables.

Cover the bottom of a pan with oil and brown chicken on one side (about 10 minutes), then flip and brown the other side (about 10 minutes). Set chicken aside. Save the oil for the sauce.

Prepare the sauce

Chop all vegetables, then add tomato, onion, green onion, celery, and bell pepper (all veggies except eggplant) to the pot.

Add the cooked vegetables set aside in Step 3 above (not the juice yet, keep saving that!)

Put a few tablespoons of the oil used to cook the chicken in Step 5 above. Cook on high heat for 5 minutes.

Add chicken, juice, water, peanut butter, eggplant, salt, and chili peppers. Simmer for about 30 minutes. Add additional salt to taste, if needed.

Eat with rice and fried or boiled plantains if you dare.

And in true Congo fashion, let me say *"Indépendance cha-cha tozui e"* (Independence cha-cha, we have won it.) Indeed.

Now about those (Cape) wines

Let me suggest a few delicious wines.

Southern Right Sauvignon Blanc, Walker Bay, South Africa. This is an elegant wine with herbs, citrus, apples, and mineral notes and an excellent finish. You cannot go wrong. Simple as that.

Raats Original Chenin Blanc, Coastal Region, South Africa. This Chenin Blanc is crafted without any oak—my kind of wine.

Edgebaston "The Pepper Pot" Red, Stellenbosch, South Africa. I thought this was a great wine all around.

SOUTH AFRICA

Ostrich Pie, which is Best Served at 3500 feet Above Sea-Level

Ostrich Pie

Serves: 6-8

Cooking time: 25 minutes

Ingredients

3 T olive oil
2 T butter
Two onions, chopped
2 kg ostrich steaks, cubed
Six fresh thyme twigs
2 cups quality beef stock
Ground cloves
Ground coriander
Ground cinnamon
4 T blackcurrant jam
2 T redcurrant jelly
3 T port (or apple jam) and black pepper, to taste
Two rolls of puff pastry

Directions

Catch your ostrich.

Heat oven to 220°C

Heat olive oil and butter with thyme, and sauté onions and ostrich.

Add stock and simmer with lid on for about 2 hours or until soft. Let cool, then flake the meat. Add spices, blackcurrant jam, redcurrant jelly, and port (or apple juice). Season to taste.

Place a layer of puff pastry on a baking tray and cut a third of the way down on either side to make strips.

Spread the filling down the center and pleat the strips over, as shown in the photo.

Repeat for the second pie.

Bake for about 20 – 25 minutes until golden brown, then slice and serve with redcurrant or quince jelly.

Now about those wines
Vriesenhof Pinot Noir
Vergelegen Sauvignon Blanc, Western Cape
Bouchard Finlayson Galpin Peak Pinot Noir
Cape Point Vineyards Sauvignon Blanc

INDIA

Easy Indian Butter Chicken- Delhi Style

Namaste everyone!

I recently returned from an extended business trip to India. Business, yes, but I must confess I did steal a few moments for myself while in Delhi, Hyderabad, Mumbai, Chennai, Bangalore, and Kolkata (at least planned.) I ate well, as one does quite often in India. I cannot begin to recall all the dishes I so eagerly sampled, but their flavors and delightful aromas remain a powerful memory, seared forever in my soul.

Here is one of the more popular Indian dishes, which rumor has originated from a famous old restaurant in Delhi. I found it impossible not to fall in love with this dish; its rich and silky sauce is to die for. When I first tasted this dish, I became a devoted follower. I am sure someone will tell me how I could even dismiss the other popular dishes like the Hyderabadi Chicken Biryani. While a tasty dish, I find butter chicken more to my liking but maybe not to my waistline. Ah, the sacrifices one must make in life.

Indian Butter Chicken
(Such a delicious dish!)

Ingredients
(Serves 4-6)
Two tablespoons of lemon juice
One teaspoon of Garam Masala Powder
One tablespoon Ginger-Garlic Paste
One teaspoon of Tandoori Masala
Salt, to taste.
2 pounds boneless, skinless chicken
1 cup Makhani Masala
Two tablespoons ghee
One tablespoon of brown sugar
1/2 cup heavy cream
One tablespoon of *kasuri methi* (dried fenugreek leaves, also known as *mentha*.) Fear not if your local food store does not carry

this; a substitute to consider is spinach or dried mustard greens, or collard greens. You are now ready.

Directions

Preheat the oven to 350 degrees. Mix the lemon juice, Garam Masala, Ginger-Garlic Paste, Tandoori Masala, and one teaspoon of salt in a large mixing bowl. Add the chicken.

Mix, then transfer to a baking dish and bake for 10 minutes. Note: You may wish to marinate the chicken for at least half an hour before baking it in the oven. Just saying.

Transfer the baked chicken to the slow cooker (discard extra liquid). Add the Makhani Masala and the other ingredients except for the heavy cream and *kasuri methi" mum."* Adjust salt as needed. Mix well, cover, and cook on high for 2 hours or low for 4 hours.

Add heavy cream and *kasuri methi.* Stir well. Cover and cook on high for another twenty minutes or until the chicken is cooked and you can no longer stand the delightful aromas. Serve with Naan (buttered garlic Naan please) and simple steamed rice.

What to drink with butter chicken, you ask? May I suggest a nice cold bottle of Kingfisher Indian beer? Nothing better.

Bombay Chicken

Ingredients
1-1/2 cups plain yogurt
¼ cup lemon juice
Two tablespoons of chili powder
Two tablespoons paprika
Two tablespoons of olive oil
1-1/2 teaspoons salt
½ to 1 teaspoon of cayenne pepper
½ teaspoon garlic powder
¼ teaspoon ground ginger
¼ teaspoon cardamom
1/8 teaspoon cinnamon
4 – 5 pounds bone-in chicken thighs and legs, skin removed

Directions
In a large shallow dish, combine all ingredients except the chicken. Add the chicken; turn to coat. Refrigerate and cover overnight, then drain the chicken, discarding the marinade.

On a lightly oiled grill rack, grill chicken, covered, over medium-hot heat for 10-15 minutes on each side or until a thermometer reads 170°-175°.

What to drink with this yummy dish?
My first thought would be to grab a cold Kingfisher beer. After all, this is a super casual meal, and Kingfisher is the king of beers.

MADRAS-STYLE FISH CURRY

This is a Chennai-style fish curry that is spicy and tangy, and delicious. Not something you should attempt to make an hour ahead of your dinner guests arriving. Just saying.

Many thanks to Yaarthi and *yummytummyaarthi.com*

Ingredients

For marinating:
Fish – 500 grams
Chili Powder – 2 tsp
Turmeric Powder/*Manjal Podi* – 1 tsp
Salt – 1 tsp
For the masala:
Oil – ¼ cup
Mustard Seeds/ *Kaduku* – 1 tsp
Fenugreek Seeds – ¼ tsp
Dry Red Chili – 2
Curry leaves – use a small handful.
Onions – 2 large chopped finely
Tomatoes – 3 large chopped finely
Green Chili – 2
Chili Powder – 1 tbsp.
Kashmiri Chili Powder – 3 tbsp.
Coriander Powder / *Malli Podi* – 2 tbsp.
Turmeric Powder / *Manjal Podi* – 2 tsp
Tamarind – 2tbsp or one small gooseberry
Salt to taste
Coriander leaves a small handful finely chopped.
Water as needed.

Instructions

Take fish and the marinating spices and mix well. Set it aside.

Soak tamarind in water, squeeze them well, strain them, and set them aside. Heat an earthenware pot, add oil, and crackle in mustard, fenugreek, dry chili, and curry leaves.

Add onions and green chilies. Add salt and mix well. Cook until it gets lightly translucent.

Add in tomatoes and cook until it gets mushy; add the spice powders and a splash of water and mix well. Cook until oil separates.

Now add tamarind water and salt. Add more water as needed. Please bring it to a boil.

Add fish and mix well. Bring it to a boil again and simmer for 10 to 15 minutes. Add in fresh curry leaves and coriander leaves.

Mix well and serve over rice. Enjoy!

Now about those wines.

What to drink with a spicy dish like this?

A Sauvignon Blanc (New Zealand, Marlborough preferably) or the casual go-to, a nice cold bottle of Kingfisher Indian beer. Nothing better.

About the Author

Richard Rogers is a third-generation francophone who grew up in Paris in the 1950s and 1960s. His family has had an association with France since 1912.

In his first book, *A Long Look Back: A Sentimental Journey of an American Growing up in France,* the author writes about themes he is deeply passionate about. He recalls his boyhood days in Paris and the long, seemingly endless summers spent at the old family house in Brittany. Those summers were set against the region's picturesque, rugged coastline and emerald-blue waters. This richness and colorfulness remain, for the author, a never-ending source of inspiration and deep sentimentality.

In his latest book, *A Foreign Port of Entry*, the author brings a different but equally rich international perspective. One based on his extensive travels to more than two dozen countries on five continents with more than seventy visits, all in a relatively short period. As a writer, he is passionate about the visual, cultural, and historical richness of cities such as Hanoi and Cape Town, Istanbul, and Cairo.

He departs briefly from his global travels and recalls the tumultuous years growing up in Congo, the Heart of Darkness. It was then, very much a young country, free from its colonial masters yet internally divided by political strife, attempted coups, and assassinations. Global powers, the United States and, at that time, the Soviet Union, sought to control the country's precious strategic resources. For the author, those adolescent years in Congo were tremendously impactful. He has compiled a collection of anecdotes and stories from his formative years in Congo.

Join the author for an open-air, late-midnight dinner in Chengdu hosted by ever-smiling local CCP officials. Fiery-hot strips of Sichuan beef washed down with repeated shots of a local, high-octane drink.

Take a ferry ride crossing the Bosphorus from Istanbul's European to the Asian side, where the author joins a customer for a beautiful seafood dinner. Istanbul was once a favorite haunt of legendary British double agent Kim Philby and the best-known master spy, James Bond. In Istanbul, it's best to watch your back and trust no one.

In A Foreign Port of Entry, the author blends mystery, intrigue, storytelling, and humor with unique cuisines from far-flung exotic cultures in shaping this exciting adventure. It is a testament to the transformative powers of travel and the beauty that exists in our world.

A Long Look Back: A Sentimental Journey Of An American Growing Up In France
December 2023

Available on Amazon

An entertaining, often humorous, sentimental journey set first in the rugged and beautiful Emerald Coast of Brittany, then in Paris, concluding with a collection of unique travel and delicious food experiences as the author meanders down from Lyon to the Côte d'Azur.

A Long, Look Back is an undeniably wonderful, warm-hearted, tender journey into a France of yesteryear.

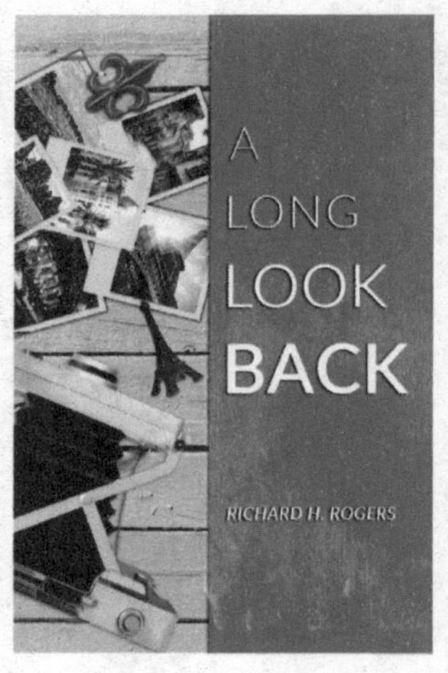

A Love of France and Food	Lovely Memoir of Childhood in France
"The author's love of France comes through in short stories of growing up as part of an ex-pat family. If you need a primer on food in various departments of France, it's here, plus some recipes full of tasty calories. This is a book that you can sit down and read a little bit at a time to satisfy the Francophile in you." LW April 2023	"I greatly enjoyed reading this memoir of an American boy and his family growing up in France in the 1950s. The evocation of his "happy place" in Bretagne, where they owned a house and spent summers, was detailed and evocative. Best of all were the descriptions of the meals that Rogers remembers from his childhood. He even includes recipes!" JC December 2022.